Children's Rooms

Sally Walton has written many books on crafts and decorating techniques, including *The Home Front Guide to Doing Up Your Period Home*. Sally originally trained as a graphic designer. Stewart Walton is a renowned paint effects and decorating expert who has made television appearances around the world. Stewart created a best-selling range of stencils, stamp designs and painted furniture patterns for his company, Paintability, which he runs with Jocasta Innes. Both Sally and Stewart contribute regularly to the BBC's *Home Front*. They live by the sea in Hastings, East Sussex, with their four children.

home front

Children's Rooms

STEWART AND SALLY WALTON

BBC Books

For our children; their friends; our friends
and their children. With love.

Photographs: Bruce Hemming
Illustrations: Claire Davies

This book is published to accompany the
BBC Television series *Home Front*.

Series Producer: Mary Sackville-West
Editor: Daisy Goodwin

This edition produced for The Book People Ltd, Hall Wood
Avenue, Haydock, St Helens,
WA11 9UL by BBC Books, an imprint of BBC Worldwide
Publishing, BBC Worldwide Limited,
Woodlands, 80 Wood Lane, London W12 OTT.

First published 1998
Reprinted 1999

ISBN 0 563 38389 5

Edited and designed for BBC Books
by Phoebus Editions Ltd

Set in Futura
Printed and bound in France by Imprimerie Pollina s.a.
Colour separations by Imprimerie Pollina s.a.
Cover printed by Imprimerie Pollina s.a.

Contents

Foreword   6
Introduction   7

THE MAKEOVERS   10

The Baby's Room   12
Wall treatment   18
Appliquéd Curtains   20
Screen   24

The Toddler's Room   28
Wall treatment   34
Peg rail   36
Pinboard   37
Cupboard   38

The Little Girl's Room   42
Sink curtains   48
Wall treatment   50
Dressing table stool   54

The Teenager's Room   56
Window shutters   62
Pinboard   64
Other storage   68

THE ESSENTIALS   70

Beds   72
Floors   76
Walls   78
Windows   80
Storage   82
Lighting   86
Work surfaces   88
Safety   90

Useful addresses   92
Acknowledgements   95
Index   96

Foreword

Decorating children's rooms is a subject that we feel well qualified to tackle for *Home Front*, having four children of our own who have no hesitation in telling us exactly what they think. We put the problems to our small experts and followed some of their advice.

The first children's rooms that we decorated for *Home Front* were for Victoria (13) and Luis (5) in the first complete house make-over we tackled with the Walsh family in Pudsey. Luis wanted to live in an aquarium and his older sister longed for privacy and sophistication. Those episodes are now a part of the *Home Front* legend and parents everywhere are hoping that one of them remains firmly under lock and key because this was when Stewart taught Luis how to make fishy sponge stamps and do his own decorating! The episode featuring Victoria's room was followed by a huge mailbag of letters from

youngsters asking if we would please come and do the same for them. This book comes as a response to all those requests. We hope that it will inspire you to experiment with your own ideas but most of all we hope you will have as much fun as we did when we decorated these rooms.

Introduction

Decorating children's rooms is an on-going thing – you start before they are born, in full control of the situation, and from the moment they arrive their influence makes itself felt. *Home Front Children's Rooms* takes a look at four real rooms and gets to grips with their decorative possibilities. The book begins with a room for a new baby then goes on to the pre-schoolers, the primary-school child and finally the teenager. We find out the needs of each age-group and look at the most practical, economical and, of course, the most stylish ways to tackle the decorating. This is a book to inspire and inform, filled with

ABOVE: THESE COUNTRY COTTAGE CURTAINS ARE A MOVABLE MURAL THAT WILL ADD CHARACTER TO ANY ROOM. EASY TO MAKE AND A GOOD WAY TO USE UP YOUR FABRIC SCRAPS.

colour photographs. Befores and afters, step-by-step projects and plenty of good ideas and sound advice are offered in the spirit of the *Home Front* programme – accessible but innovative and affordable style.

NEST-BUILDING

Two weeks after your baby is born, you look around at the soft downy nest that you created to discover that it is littered with mountains of disposable nappies, wipes, lotions, potions, more washing than you usually generate in a week and enough fluffy toys to fill a small truck.

This first chapter of the book will guide you through the realities of what a baby's room needs without diminishing any of the pleasure that you get from starting afresh and decorating a room as a nursery.

But in no time at all you find that your previously stationary baby is standing, then crawling and starting to move about. Life is now all about reaching up, climbing out, falling over and spilling things. By this stage you need to consider safety features and your child needs soft landings and plenty of entertainment on his own level.

ON THE TODDLER TRAIL

This is the time to get into child-friendly storage systems – quick ways to make floor space for

ABOVE: WE MADE A SIMPLE DRESSING TABLE FROM STAIR SPINDLES AND PINE SHELVING. THE SEAT IS AN OLD PIANO STOOL, RE-COVERED AND PAINTED TO MATCH.

games without mixing up all the different types of tracks, building systems and puzzle pieces. Small kids can be creative without being chaotic, but they need some adult guidance and encouragement – so we show you how to give them space and inspiration with ideas such as a peg rail and a pinboard. We look at the way you can make the two- to five-year-old's room both a stimulating place to play and a comforting place to sleep.

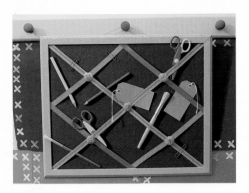

ABOVE: THIS LIVELY PINBOARD FOR THE TODDLER'S ROOM KEEPS ART EQUIPMENT AT THE READY.

PEER PRESSURE

When children start school your influence starts to wane. The combined influence of new friends and television advertising can seriously affect their attitudes. Independent little boys and girls may well reject their 'babyish' rooms and begin to have ideas of their own about colour schemes, tidiness and displays of things that interest them. Minor changes, such as a different colour on the walls, new lampshades and a few cushions can be enough to satisfy short-lived crazes without actually succumbing to the merchandising.

INTO DOUBLE FIGURES

Kids are discerning consumers by the time that they're teenagers. But many recognize that personal style extends beyond the clothes you wear to the environment you choose to live in. In this chapter we introduce some youth culture – this is the last time that you'll decorate with them, so go with the flow. Get together with scrapbooks, swatches and colour cards. Let them decide the look they want, then involve them in budgeting, any practical compromises and the actual hands-on decorating. It's important for them to experience the reality of the hard work needed and the satisfaction of a job well done; then they can, as we say on *Home Front,* stand back and admire!

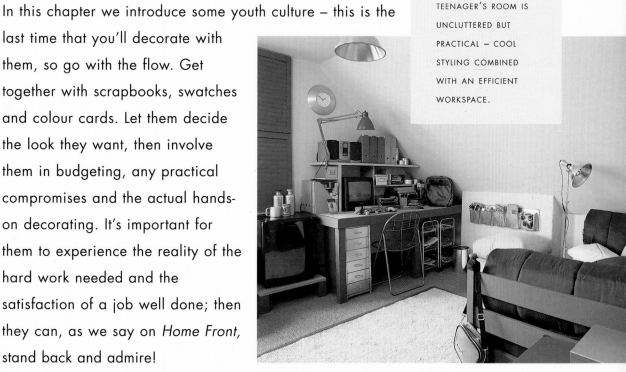

BELOW: THE TEENAGER'S ROOM IS UNCLUTTERED BUT PRACTICAL – COOL STYLING COMBINED WITH AN EFFICIENT WORKSPACE.

THE BABY'S ROOM 12

THE TODDLER'S ROOM 28

THE LITTLE GIRL'S ROOM 42

THE TEENAGER'S ROOM 56

The Makeovers

In this section we have applied bright ideas to four real, typical bedrooms. Three had inherited too much clutter and too many styles to have a distinctive character. The other was brand new but needed softening to welcome a new baby. Many of the projects will work well for the room of a child of a different age or sex. so dip in and find the ideas that appeal to you most.

The baby's room is in a country cottage that had been
newly built to an old design. Although the room has
plenty of interesting features, the new hard edges
needed softening. Colourwashing and
stamping did the trick.

The
Baby's
Room

BELOW: THE SPARE ROOM HAD JUST BEEN
DECORATED WHEN THE OWNERS DISCOVERED
THAT A NEW BABY WAS ON THE WAY.

Let's face it, new babies don't mind what their rooms look like. As long as they have a soft space to sleep in and you are within yelling distance, they are happy.

In the early days, a newborn's room needs to be a reassuring environment in which to grow. However, as babies' senses awaken and they become more aware, the challenge is to provide enough decoration to stimulate an interest in their surroundings – but not to the extent that they cannot relax. Be warned, parents should not be surprised by a baby who does not settle in a room decorated with grinning acrobatic clowns dressed in primary colours! In general, these colourful, exciting rooms are best kept for later on when the theory is that your child will be so active during the day that he will sleep like a log at night.

THE EARLY MONTHS

In the first weeks, babies spend very little time in their own bedrooms, but this is the place where all their equipment is kept. Although they are really small, babies do have a lot of belongings. The main person you need to consider in these early weeks is yourself – how far you have to bend to change a nappy and how high you have to reach to grab a sleep suit or a cot sheet.

For the first three months, babies can be found exactly where you left them. But don't become complacent – they learn to roll in an instant and are immediate experts. For this early period, you can afford to make your life easier by using visible storage like wicker baskets on low shelves filled with baby clothes, toiletries, towels and nappies – all close to hand and easy to spot. Once babies start to move, however, pulling things off shelves becomes a sport – and a dangerous one at that – so you will quickly have to move things higher up out of their reach.

SHARING ROOMS

Not everyone has a room that can be decorated for the exclusive use of a baby – he might be sharing with a sibling or occupying a corner of your

ABOVE: PARENTS NEED PAMPERING TOO, SO WE PROVIDED A COMFY ROCKING CHAIR, A SMALL TABLE AND A READING LAMP.

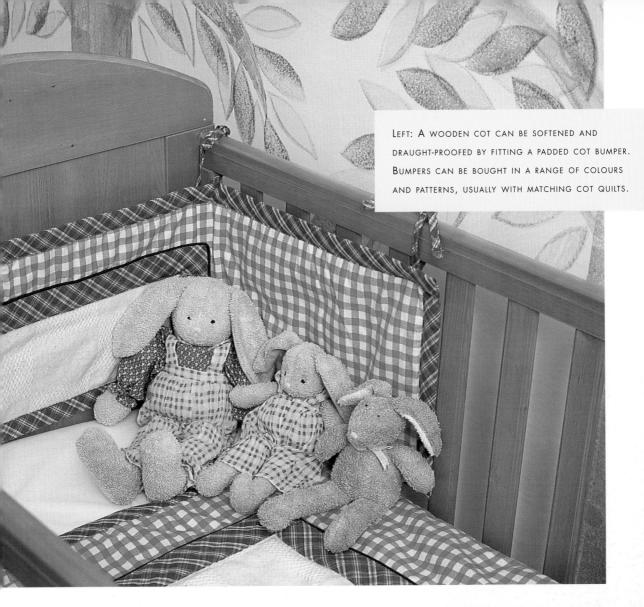

LEFT: A WOODEN COT CAN BE SOFTENED AND DRAUGHT-PROOFED BY FITTING A PADDED COT BUMPER. BUMPERS CAN BE BOUGHT IN A RANGE OF COLOURS AND PATTERNS, USUALLY WITH MATCHING COT QUILTS.

own room. We have tried to address both of these situations when designing the projects for this chapter.

The baby changer can be fitted onto an existing chest of drawers and lifted off when not in use, while the folding screen can be used around the cot to provide a little privacy for the other occupants of the room. Once the cot is screened off, a toddler will soon feel that he has regained his own space – out of sight, out of mind.

RIGHT: LAMBSKIN FLEECES ARE KNOWN TO COMFORT AND SOOTHE BABIES. THESE WASHABLE FLEECES PROVIDE A SOFT, COSY AREA FOR THE BABY TO SIT AND PLAY.

RIGHT: PRINTING WITH SPONGE STAMPS GIVES A
RANGE IN DEPTH OF COLOUR INTENSITY WHICH,
ESPECIALLY WHEN SLIGHTLY OVERPRINTED, CAN CREATE
A THREE-DIMENSIONAL EFFECT. THE FADED CHALKY
TINTING IS IDEAL FOR THIS LARGE TREE PATTERN WHICH
WOULD BE FAR TOO DOMINATING IF PRINTED IN
BRIGHTER, MORE SOLID COLOURS.

DECORATIVE THEMES

If you choose to decorate your nursery walls with a mural, we suggest using strong colours applied in a 'soft' way instead of pastel tints, which are made by adding a small amount of colour pigment to white paint and give a totally opaque finish, or flat bright areas. Try diluting rich colours with either wallpaper paste or PVA glue and water (the proportions of each appear in the project notes) and applying the mixture as a background colourwash onto a white wall, or as a pattern applied with sponges or stencils. The richer tone and softer edges that these mixtures produce are much more suited to the skills of the occasional painter than slick, outlined blocks of flat colour, which are best left to professional mural artists.

When choosing fabric for a baby's room, it is tempting to think only in the present and go for something cute and babyish. But babies grow quickly and soon look out of place surrounded by delicate pastel prints. Patchwork and appliqué look very effective in babies' rooms and are an excellent way of using up scraps of fabric and ribbon.

LIGHTING

Lighting is all important in a baby's room, and you will need to include several different kinds. A small wall-mounted or clip-on spotlight, angled towards the 'business end' – but not to shine in the little one's eyes – is perfect task lighting. It is also useful to have a bright central light to illuminate the

ABOVE: A SCREEN IS REALLY USEFUL IN A ROOM WHERE THE BABY IS SHARING WITH PARENTS OR SIBLINGS. HERE, IT HAS BEEN PLACED AROUND THE COT TO CREATE A TRANQUIL SLEEPING AREA.

whole room, but fit a dimmer switch to turn the light down low at night. If you have a comfortable chair for feeding time, a reading lamp is a good idea – not only for the novels you plan to read, but for instructions on tubes and bottles.

All things considered, it is important that you enjoy your nest building and create a place where you feel happy and comfortable spending time with your baby. It is bound to look chaotic at times, but don't despair – with a realistically large laundry basket, a waste bin and some well planned storage space, things can soon be sorted out.

Wall treatment

We used sponge stamps to paint this tree mural onto a colourwashed background. The shapes are quite large and they should encourage even the most inhibited of decorators to relax and enjoy themselves. As each shape is added, the picture grows, and by keeping the colour application light the large trees do not overpower the room. We have allowed enough spaces between the trees for you to add more creatures later on – when the creative mood strikes!

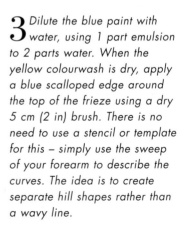

YOU WILL NEED... *Emulsion paint in your chosen colours (we used wheat yellow for the colourwashed background and mid-blue for the scalloped edge) • 2 paint kettles • A large household paintbrush (choose one 10–12 cm/4–6 in wide, depending on your capacity to hold it) • A 5 cm (2 in) household paintbrush*

PAINTING THE BACKGROUND

1 *Start by mixing the two dilutions of paint for the colourwashed background in separate paint kettles. We used a pale colour containing 1 part yellow emulsion to 4 parts water, and a darker shade containing 1 part yellow emulsion to 2 parts water.*

Beginning near the top of the wall with the palest dilution, apply the paint with a large paintbrush in broad sweeping strokes.

TIP

Work in a random way, mopping up any drips with the paintbrush as you go along and working them back into the wall to avoid streaks.

2 *Halfway down the wall, change to the darker colour and work over your last brushstrokes to blend the two together. Continue to the skirting, using the sweep of your forearm to make the hill shapes. Don't try to blend away all the brushstrokes – they add interest and keep the effect fresh and spontaneous. A mixture of light and heavy strokes adds energy and movement.*

3 *Dilute the blue paint with water, using 1 part emulsion to 2 parts water. When the yellow colourwash is dry, apply a blue scalloped edge around the top of the frieze using a dry 5 cm (2 in) brush. There is no need to use a stencil or template for this – simply use the sweep of your forearm to describe the curves. The idea is to create separate hill shapes rather than a wavy line.*

ABOVE: THIS CLOSE-UP DETAIL
EMPHASIZES HOW LIGHTLY THE COLOUR
IS APPLIED. IT ALSO SHOWS HOW THE
LEAF SHAPES SHOULD OVERLAP.

ABOVE: THIS CLOSE-UP DETAIL
EMPHASIZES HOW LIGHTLY THE COLOUR
IS APPLIED. IT ALSO SHOWS HOW THE
LEAF SHAPES SHOULD OVERLAP.

YOU WILL NEED...

Paper • Spray adhesive • 4
pieces of foam, 2.5 cm (1 in)
thick – washing-up sponge is
ideal • A craft knife or scalpel
• Emulsion paints (we used a
mixture of Cobalt Blue and
Raw Umber for the blue
leaves; Cadmium Yellow and
Raw Sienna for the yellow
leaves; Indian Red for the leaf
outlines; and green made by
mixing the Cobalt Blue and
Cadium Yellow for the grass
and birds

APPLYING THE SPONGED MOTIFS

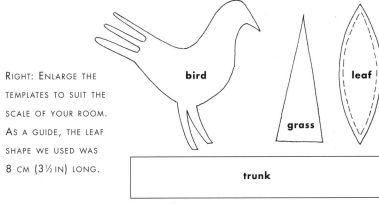

RIGHT: ENLARGE THE
TEMPLATES TO SUIT THE
SCALE OF YOUR ROOM.
AS A GUIDE, THE LEAF
SHAPE WE USED WAS
8 CM (3½ IN) LONG.

1 Apply a light coat of spray
adhesive to the back of
each paper template and stick
down on separate pieces of
foam. Following the outline of
the templates with a craft knife,
cut out the shape. Remove the
waste foam and paper.

2 Starting at the base of the
frieze, stamp on the grass
using the triangular stamp and
green paint. Next use the
rectangular brick shape to stamp
the tree trunk. When you reach
the top, divide the trunk into six
branch shapes and use the same
rectangular stamp to paint the
branches. As you reach the end
of each branch, turn the sponge
on its side to get a finer shape.
Use the leaf stamp to apply a
generous number of leaves in
both colours.

3 When you are pleased with
the amount of foliage, use
a scalpel to cut out the inside of
the leaf stamp. You should be
left with a narrow outline shape.
Use this to overprint every leaf.

4 Position the birds in
different positions on the
mural – one on a branch, one
among the foliage, and one on
the ground.

Appliquéd curtains

TIP

When measuring the curtain panels, do not make them too full or the shape of the cottage will be lost in the folds.

These curtains may look terribly ambitious, but they are not at all. All you need is a sewing machine that does zigzag stitch, some inexpensive fabric for the background, and plenty of scraps for the appliqué.

We have provided a detailed diagram of each panel so that you can trace off the shapes and use them as templates, but you may prefer to use them as inspiration to make up a country cottage of your own.

Once again, we have not listed the quantities of fabric needed, since the size of your curtains will depend on the shape of your window. However, it should be possible for you to adapt this pattern to fit any window. After all, country cottages are not built in one regular size – they come in many eccentric shapes and sizes.

ABOVE: THE GATHERED PELMET REPRESENTS A THATCHED ROOF, WHILE BROAD RIBBON IS USED FOR THE TIMBER BEAMS

TEMPLATE FOR THE CURTAINS

FABRICS NEEDED TO MAKE THE CURTAINS

 PAINTER'S CALICO FOR THE UPPER PANEL

 'BRICK' DESIGN FABRIC FOR THE LOWER PANEL

 YELLOW FABRIC FOR THE DOOR

 MEDIUM BLUE DENIM FOR THE RIGHT-HAND WINDOWS

DARK BLUE DENIM FOR THE LEFT-HAND WINDOWS

 BROWN PETERSHAM RIBBON, 5 CM (2 IN) WIDE, FOR THE DARK BEAMS

 CARPET BINDING TAPE, 5 CM (2 IN) WIDE, FOR THE WINDOW FRAMES

 BLUE SPOTTED FABRIC FOR THE LOWER WINDOW CURTAINS

 WHITE COTTON LACE, 7.5 CM (3 IN) AND 2.5 CM (1 IN) WIDE, TO TRIM THE LOWER WINDOW

 RED BANDANNA SCARF FOR THE FLOWERHEADS

 BLUE BANDANNA SCARF FOR THE FLOWERHEADS

 BLUE-AND-WHITE GINGHAM FOR THE CAT

 RED-AND-WHITE GINGHAM FOR THE CACTUS POT

 GREY-AND-WHITE TICKING FOR THE CACTUS

 LIGHT GREEN FELT FOR THE FLOWER STEMS AND LEAVES

 LIGHT BROWN FELT FOR THE DOVES

 LIGHT BLUE FELT FOR THE DOVES

 DARK GREY FELT FOR THE NEST

 WHITE FELT FOR THE DOVE EGGS

21

MAKING THE CURTAINS

1 Cut out the calico and 'brick' fabric for the two curtain panels. Place a piece of calico on top of a piece of 'brick' fabric, with right sides together and raw edges even. Stitch together along the top edge, then open out and press the seams to one side.

2 Cut out the door and four denim window shapes and lay them in position on the curtain panels. Pin in place.

3 Cut the petersham ribbon and carpet tape for the beams and window frames to the correct length. Pin in place on the curtain panels, taking care that they overlap the doors and windows by at least 3 mm (⅛ in).

TIP

Do not take the ribbon right up to the sides of the curtain panels; stop within 3 cm (1 in) of the raw edges to allow for seam allowances.

4 To make the curtains for the lower window, cut two pieces of spotted fabric the same width as the denim background. Neaten the four edges of each by taking a 6 mm (¼ in) hem all around.

To gather the curtains, make two parallel rows of stitching along the top edge of each curtain. Use a large stitch and loosen the tension. Gather the curtains by pulling the bobbin threads to fit the window. Pin in place on the window.

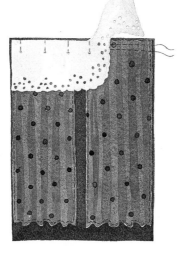

5 Cut the widest strip of lace to fit the top edge of the window and zigzag stitch in place, turning in the side edges to neaten them. Pin the narrow lace around the sides and base of the window and also use it to make a cross-bar in the centre. Zigzag stitch in place.

6 The small template shapes, such as the cactus and flowerheads, are mounted on interfacing to stiffen the fabric and prevent it from fraying. Cut a piece of interfacing for each and iron it to the reverse. The birds and flower stems are cut from felt, which does not need to be mounted on interfacing.

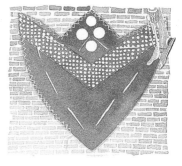

7 Following the illustration on page 21, position the fabric shapes on the curtain panels and pin, baste, then zigzag stitch in place.

TIP

Vary the width of the zigzag stitch to suit the size and shape of the pieces.

8 Once you have stitched the shapes in place, you can add the decorative details by hand or machine. The birds' legs are done with a close zigzag stitch; the buttons that are used for the cat's eyes are stitched in place by hand.

9 Cut a piece of lining fabric for each curtain panel, making it exactly the same size as the finished panel, and place right sides together. Taking a 3 cm (1 in) seam, stitch around three sides, leaving the top edge open. Trim the seams to 1.5 cm (½ in), turn right sides out and press.

10 To neaten the top edge, turn under 3 cm (1 in) towards the wrong side and press. Pin the heading tape along the top edge and stitch in place, catching the cord pulls down one side edge in the line of stitching.

MAKING THE PELMET

The pelmet is made from one metre (39 in) of corduroy, which is cut in half and rejoined edge to edge to make a double-width, half-metre (20 in) strip. The finished piece should be roughly twice the width of your window.

1 Erect a simple shelf above the curtain track using the wooden brackets to support the shelf in the centre and on either side. This should give a nice 'boxed' effect.

2 Fold the corduroy for the pelmet in half lengthways and cut along the fold. You will now have two matching full-width pieces. Join them in the centre to make one long piece and press the seam open. Stitch a hem around the bottom and side edges to neaten them. Fold under 3 cm (1 in) along the top edge and pin, then stitch the heading tape in place.

3 The pelmet is fixed to the shelf with upholsterer's tacks. Find the middle of the pelmet shelf and hammer a tack through the centre seam of the pelmet into the edge of the shelf. Gather up the pelmet to fit the shelf by pulling up the cords on the heading tape. Make sure that it is evenly pleated, then secure with tacks along its length.

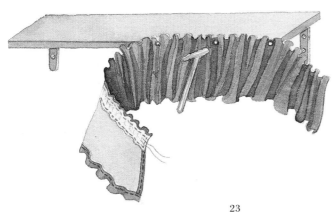

LEFT: THE SCREEN CAN BE FOLDED UP AND HOOKED TOGETHER TO MAKE A USEFUL SOFT TOY STORAGE AREA.

You Will Need...

8 lengths of 38 mm (1½ in) square prepared timber, 1.5 m (5 ft) long, for the uprights • 8 lengths of 38 mm (1½ in) square prepared timber, 50 cm (20 in) long, for the horizontals • An electric drill fitted with a countersink drill bit • Wood adhesive • A right-angled try square • 16 wood screws, 65 mm (2½ in) long • A screwdriver • Wood filler • 8 small screw-in wooden door knobs for the finials • Wood primer • A small foam roller or household paintbrush • Blue emulsion or satinwood paint in your chosen colour • 6 brass butt hinges • A bradawl • 16 screw-in hooks and eyes, for use with plastic-coated sprung wire • 5 m (5½ yds) of 91 cm- (36 in)-wide fabric for the curtain panels • 4 m (13 ft) plastic-coateld sprung wire (net curtain wire)

Screen

The screen is a multi-functional piece that is easy to make, lightweight and really useful. The hinges can be lifted apart to make two double panel screens, or the four sides can be joined to make a toy store or a play area. Our screen is quite tall, but you could make a shorter version by simply reducing the height of the timber uprights.

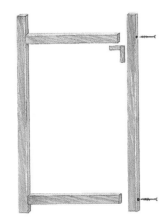

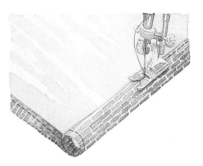

3 *Prime the four panels, then paint in your chosen colour of emulsion or satinwood paint and leave to dry.*

6 *Cut the four fabric panels to the correct size, making them twice as wide as the horizontals. Neaten the side edges by turning under a narrow hem. To make the casing for the wire at the top and bottom, first turn under 6 mm (¼ in) to the wrong side and press, then turn under 1.5 cm (½ in) to the wrong side and topstitch in place.*

1 *Start by assembling the four identical panels. Lay a timber upright on the floor and place a horizontal at right angles to one side edge, 10 cm (4 in) from the top. Place a second horizontal underneath the first, 5 cm (2 in) from the bottom. Mark the position of each, then drill pilot holes for the screws. Glue the horizontals in place, using the try square to check that your joints are 90 degrees, then fix in place with screws. Place an upright on the opposite side and fix in place in the same way. Make up three more panels.*

4 *The screen is assembled with hinges, which are fixed to the same side of each panel. Lay two panels on the floor, butting them up alongside each other. Position the hinges across the uprights, placing one just below the upper horizontals and another just above the lower horizontals. Use a bradawl to make pilot holes for the screws, then fix in place. Join the remaining panels in the same way, then hinge the two sets together.*

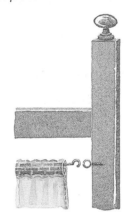

2 *Make a small pilot hole with a bradawl in the top of each upright, then screw a wooden knob in each.*

5 *Mark the position of the eye fittings on the inside edge of every upright. The first mark is 5 cm (2 in) below the upper horizontal; the second is 2.5 cm (1 in) above the lower horizontal. Use a bradawl to make a small pilot hole for each eye, then screw into the wood.*

7 *Cut eight lengths of sprung wire slightly shorter than the horizontals. This measurement is deliberately short to allow for the wires to stretch and create enough tension to hold the curtains taut. Screw a hook into either end of each piece of wire, feed the wire through the casings and attach to the screen.*

Changing unit

This is based on a similar changing unit that we saw at a friend's home many years ago. It consists of a removable tray that fits on top of an existing chest of drawers. The unit is held securely in place by a lip below the base.

YOU WILL NEED... *18 mm (¾ in) MDF for the base, front, back sides and undershelf • A handsaw • An electric drill or hand drill fitted with a countersunk bit • A jigsaw • Wood adhesive • Wood screws, 25 mm(1 in) long • A screwdriver • Wood filler (optional) • Wood primer • Satinwood paint in your chosen colour • A small foam roller or household paintbrush*

1 *Measure the top of your chest of drawers and cut a piece of MDF to the exact size. This is the base of your unit.*

3 *Cut out the two end pieces. These are rectangles, each the same depth as the chest of drawers and 15 cm (6 in) high.*

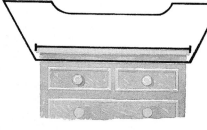

2 *Draw a base line the same length as the chest of drawers on a sheet of MDF. Mark a 30-degree angle at either end to give the slope of the sides, extending it 15 cm (6 in) above the base line and 4 cm (1½ in) below the base line. This will give the lip that is needed to hold the unit on the chest. Using this drawing as template, cut out two pieces of MDF – one for the front and one for the back. Then use a jigsaw to cut a curved section out of the front only.*

4 *To assemble the unit, butt the two sides up to the front and back pieces, mark the position of the screws, then drill pilot holes through from the front and back. Glue the pieces together, then reinforce with screws. If desired, fill the pilot holes with filler before painting.*

5 *Drop the base in from the top. It will not go all the way to the bottom. Press it in firmly, check that it is level then secure it with wood screws through the sides. Cut a small piece of wood to form a shelf at one end of the changing unit.*

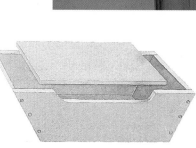

6 Prime the entire unit, inside and out, then paint in your chosen colour – we used cornflower blue. Leave to dry, then fit the changing mat and shelf inside.

TIP

When the changing unit is no longer needed, why not convert it into an under-bed storage drawer?

ABOVE: MAKE THE UNIT TO FIT ON TOP OF AN EXISTING CHEST OF DRAWERS, USING A STANDARD PLASTIC COVERED CHANGING MAT OR PRAM MATTRESS TO PAD THE INSIDE.

This room was a real challenge because it was situated
at basement level with very little natural light entering
through a small, high window. We needed to brighten
the room up and also scale things down because the
high ceiling and tall shelving felt
quite oppressive.

The
Toddler's
Room

BELOW: THE ROOM HAD BEEN INHERITED
FROM A TEENAGE BROTHER. ONCE THE
TODDLER'S THINGS WERE ADDED, IT BECAME
A CLUTTER OF UNCO-ORDINATED STYLES.

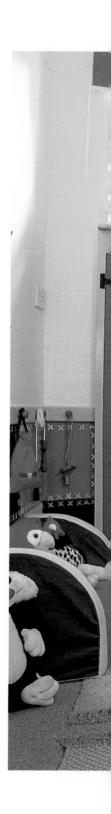

BELOW: WE BROUGHT THE ROOM DOWN TO TODDLER HEIGHT BY ADDING A LOW PEG RAIL AND FITTING STORAGE CUPBOARDS UP HIGH AND EVERYDAY CUPBOARDS WITHIN REACH. THE LITTLE BED WAS PAINTED TO MATCH THE BRILLIANT NEW COLOUR SCHEME.

ABOVE AND BELOW: THIS STUNNING BED LINEN INSPIRED THE ROOM'S DECORATING SCHEME – FROM THE PATCHWORK COLOURS ON THE WALLS TO THE CUT-OUT CROCODILE HANDLES THAT WE MADE FOR THE CUPBOARD DOORS.

Ideally, you should aim to provide an environment that is comfortable and reassuring to fall asleep in and exciting to wake up in. Children may seem full of bravado at this age, but they are still very small and need a lot of company and attention to make them feel secure. Try to see the room from their point of view by getting down on the floor with them and having a look at it from their perspective. A large room can be

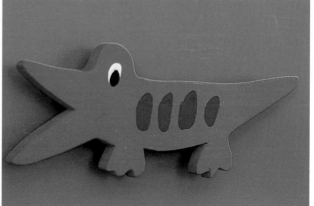

overwhelming for a small child, so where possible try to scale things down to their level. In Stephanie's room, we did this by positioning the peg rail lower than the usual dado rail height, and making her a special small-scale door (see page 36). The full-size door is still there, but has been painted to look like part of the wall.

STORAGE

Toddlers have more toys than any other age-group, and it will make a huge difference to your life if you manage to get the storage right. A toy box will not be enough – you need to provide lots of different ones for everything from train sets and building bricks to jigsaws and dolls' clothes. Stacking plastic boxes come in many sizes and colours, and if you get the transparent ones your toddler may even resist the temptation of tipping everything out to check the contents. Rumour has it that children can be trained to put away their own toys – if this is true, then a system of identifiable boxes will be a great help to them as well.

When planning the different storage areas, try to install a two-tier system, with low shelves for things that you do want them to have access to and high areas for things that you do not. This is an age of exploration and defiance, so even when you have made it crystal clear to them that certain areas are out-of-bounds, you can bet your life that the first time they have a friend around and it goes quiet, they will be emptying all the containers within their reach.

LEFT: THERE WASN'T ENOUGH FLOORSPACE FOR A CONVENTIONAL EASEL IN STEPHANIE'S ROOM, SO WE CONVERTED A SECTION OF THE CUPBOARD DOORS INTO A CHALKBOARD USING SPECIAL BLACKBOARD PAINT.

BELOW: THE CUPBOARD IS FITTED WITH FIVE SHELVES, EACH HOLDING TRANSPARENT STORAGE BOXES.

ABOVE: FOR SOMEONE WITH A GREAT FUTURE AHEAD OF HER — A LITTLE STAGE, FITTED WITH MIRRORS, A SPOTLIGHT AND A FANCY SET OF DRAPES.

THE FRAME FOR THE STAGE CONSISTS OF A RECTANGULAR BOX, WHICH WAS BUILT ACROSS THE CORNER OF THE ROOM. THE STAGE ITSELF IS MADE FROM A SHEET OF THE THICKEST MDF (32 MM/ 1¼ IN), WHICH FITS ON TOP OF THE FRAME AND PROVIDES ROOM FOR STORING DRESSING UP CLOTHES UNDERNEATH. ADDITIONAL STORAGE IS CONCEALED IN THE CORNER CUPBOARD, WHICH IS FITTED WITH NARROW SHELVES AND MIRROR DOORS.

DECORATIVE THEMES

Your own child is bound to have a particular interest that you can indulge when deciding on a decorative theme. Our corner stage came from Stephanie and her friends' delight in dressing up and dancing, but you could easily adapt the idea to make a shop, space ship, playhouse or castle turret for a princess.

DEALING WITH SMALL SPACES

If the room that you are decorating is very small, there are many ways to give it a more spacious feel. Invest in a child-sized bed, instead of the normal 2 m (6 ft 6 in) length, to make the most of available floor space. And move the storage up high onto shelves, or install a set of fitted kitchen cupboards. If you angle the lighting down into the play area, the storage will not be noticed. This is where dual-purpose furniture comes into its own, so invest in a built-in bench down one side of the room and either fit curtains underneath or fix upward hinging doors along the front to hide storage boxes of toys and games. When you need an instant clear-up, you can sweep everything into this space and deal with it later.

LIGHTING

If your room has high ceilings, lighting is a good way of visually lowering the boundaries without doing any structural work. If you use a central light, hang it lower than you would normally and use a coolie-style shade to spread the light outwards and downwards. A dimmer switch is useful to either calm or brighten the whole room in an instant. High cupboards won't be much good if you can't see their contents, and these are best lit with small striplights. Wall mounted spotlights provide good direct light and are ideal for the main activity areas. Table lamps are useful for night-time reading, but these should be fixed securely to a surface or they present a

LEFT: WE TRANSFORMED THE TABLE LAMP BY PAINTING THE SHADE WITH THE SAME GREEN PAINT THAT WE USED FOR THE PINBOARD (AFTER CONVERTING IT FIRST FOR USE WITH FABRIC). WE THEN OVERSTITCHED THE EDGES WITH RED WOOL TO MATCH THE COLOUR OF THE BASE AND TRIMMED THE BOTTOM WITH POMPONS.

fire hazard. If you're worried about this, fix a wall-mounted reading light with a guard instead.

Decorating for toddlers should be tremendous fun. They will be thrilled by your efforts, so get into the spirit of it.

ABOVE: THE HIGH WINDOW NEEDED BRIGHTENING, SO WE FILLED AN INDOOR WINDOW BOX WITH FISH TANK GRAVEL AND FLOWERS THAT WILL NEVER WILT.

Wall treatment

We took our inspiration for this vibrant wall treatment from the patchwork quilt on the bed, and used a similar selection of very bright colours. To get the feel of a handmade fabric patchwork, we staggered the blocks of colour in two rows all the way round the lower half of the room.

The little 'kisses', or cross-stitch borders, are made using a sponge stamp. This sort of decorating should be fun to do and makes a good group activity – so cut out a few stamps, put on some music and get into the rhythm of repeat patterns. Don't be a perfectionist – go for a hand-printed look with stamps that vary in intensity.

YOU WILL NEED...
A pencil • A spirit level • A medium-sized household paintbrush • Emulsion paint (we used scenic paints for their intensity) • Paper • Spray adhesive • A small square of dense foam or sponge, 2.5 cm (1 in) thick • A craft knife or scalpel • White emulsion paint • Water-based acrylic matt varnish to seal (optional)

1 *Use a pencil to mark the patchwork effect on the walls. A spirit level is useful to check the verticals and horizontals, but draw the lines free-hand to imitate the cut edge of a fabric patchwork. Note that the blocks are slightly stepped, not lined up with one another.*

2 *Fill in the blocks with a paintbrush. Work on one colour at a time, starting with the palest colour and progressing to the darker ones. Precision is not important here – in fact, a wavy line is preferable for a hand-finished look.*

3 *Trace off the cross shape for the stamp onto a sheet of paper. Trim the edges slightly and glue onto the foam. Use a craft knife to cut out the stamp to a depth of about 1 cm (½ in). Discard any waste foam.*

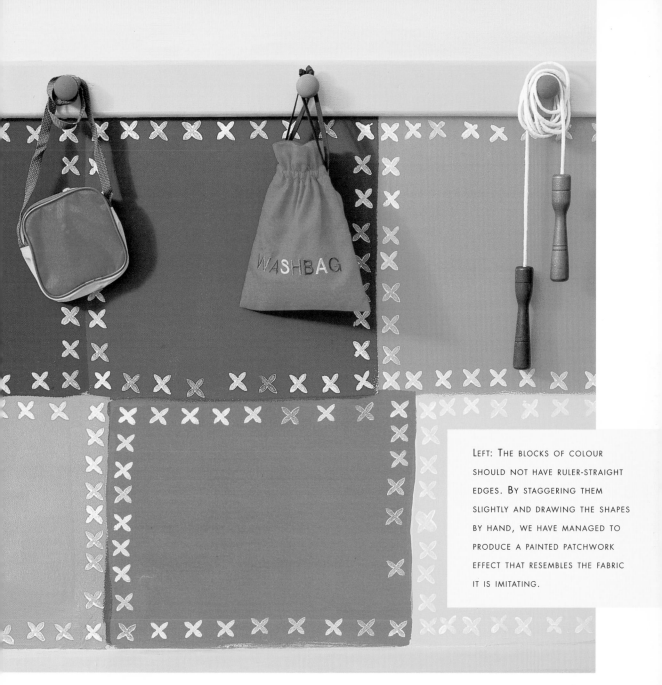

LEFT: THE BLOCKS OF COLOUR
SHOULD NOT HAVE RULER-STRAIGHT
EDGES. BY STAGGERING THEM
SLIGHTLY AND DRAWING THE SHAPES
BY HAND, WE HAVE MANAGED TO
PRODUCE A PAINTED PATCHWORK
EFFECT THAT RESEMBLES THE FABRIC
IT IS IMITATING.

4 Apply white emulsion to the stamp with a brush, then stamp the cross-stitch border around the outside of every block. A loaded stamp will print 3–4 times. Leave to dry. If desired, seal the walls with acrylic varnish.

Peg rail

Thanks to the Shakers and their furnishing style, we all understand how useful a peg rail can be. This one is made from lengths of pine batten fitted with small wooden door knobs, which we painted in different colours to match the decoration of the room.

   The rail is fixed at a much lower height than the usual dado rail, so that it is within easy reach of the toddler.

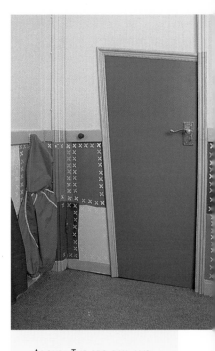

YOU WILL NEED... *A pencil • A tape measure • A spirit level attached to a ruler • 7.5 x 2.5 cm (3 x 1 in) batten to fit around the room as a rail • A small hand saw • A mitre-block (optional) • Wood filler (optional) • A small household paintbrush • White acrylic primer • Emulsion paint in your chosen colours (we used scenic paints for their intensity) • Screw-in wooden door knobs • A bradawl • An electric drill fitted with a 7mm masonry bit • Brown wall plugs • Gauge 10 chipboard screws, 75 mm (3 in) long • A screwdriver*

1 *Start by marking the position of the peg rail on the wall, using a pencil and a spirit level attached to a ruler. This one is 75 cm (30 in) high.*

2 *Cut the wooden battens to fit around the room. We mitred the corners using a mitring block, but you can simply butt the battens up against each other if you prefer and fill in any gaps with wood filler before painting.*

3 *Paint the wooden battens first with white acrylic primer, then with your chosen colour. Also prime and paint the wooden door knobs. We chose primary colours to co-ordinate with the walls.*

4 *The battens are fixed to the wall with rawlplugs and screws. Start by making pilot holes in the lengths of batten, spacing them at intervals of 60 cm (24 in). Position the batten on the wall, insert the drill bit into a pilot hole and drill through the wood into the wall. You can now remove the batten, insert the rawlplugs into the wall and fix the battens with screws.*

ABOVE: THE PEG RAIL AND THE SPECIALLY CUT-DOWN DOOR-WITHIN-A-DOOR ARE DELIBERATELY DESIGNED TO BE AT TODDLER-HEIGHT.

5 *Mark the position of the knobs along the peg rail and make pilot holes with a bradawl. To fix in place, simply screw the knobs into the rail with your hand.*

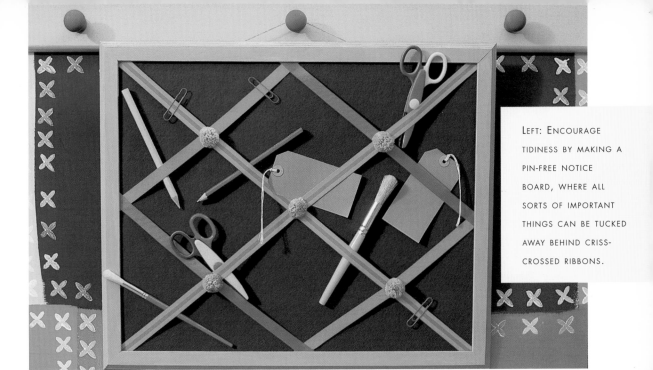

LEFT: ENCOURAGE TIDINESS BY MAKING A PIN-FREE NOTICE BOARD, WHERE ALL SORTS OF IMPORTANT THINGS CAN BE TUCKED AWAY BEHIND CRISS-CROSSED RIBBONS.

Pinboard

This idea is based on the old-fashioned notice boards that used a grid of criss-crossed ribbons on a fabric background. No drawing pins are needed, making it a safe and easy way to display everything from postcards and party invitations to photographs and pictures. We used an ordinary picture frame for the surround and backing, so no carpentry skills are required.

YOU WILL NEED...
A large frame • Emulsion paint in your chosen colour (we used lime green scenic paint for its intensity) • A small household paintbrush • Felt for the backing • Clear adhesive • Brightly coloured petersham ribbon, 12 mm (½ in) wide, or elastic if preferred • A staple gun • Coloured pompons

2 Cut a piece of blue felt the same size as the hardboard backing and attach to the backing with clear glue. Allow to dry.

3 Run two pieces of ribbon diagonally across the felt backing, from corner to corner. Use a staple gun to secure them at the edges and where they intersect in the middle. Add four more pieces of ribbon from the middle of each side and staple in place.

4 To finish, glue a pompon at every intersection and leave to dry. Reassemble the frame, omitting the glass.

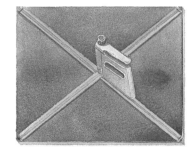

1 Remove the glass and hardboard backing from the frame. Paint the surround in your chosen colour and leave to dry.

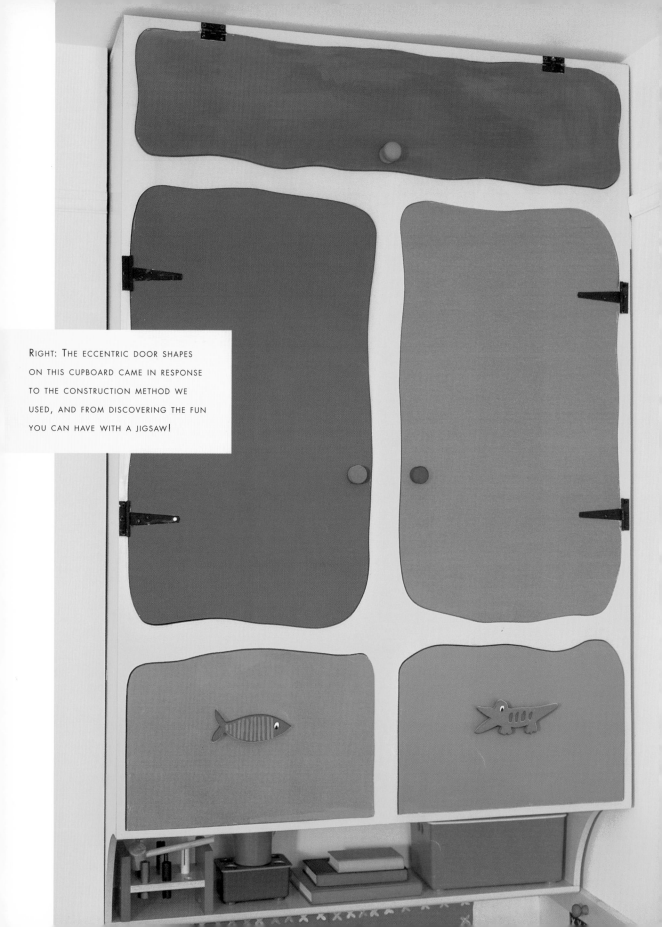

RIGHT: THE ECCENTRIC DOOR SHAPES
ON THIS CUPBOARD CAME IN RESPONSE
TO THE CONSTRUCTION METHOD WE
USED, AND FROM DISCOVERING THE FUN
YOU CAN HAVE WITH A JIGSAW!

Cupboard

It might sound rather over-ambitious to make a built-in cupboard from scratch, but this isn't cabinet-making – it's more like fitting a basic box into an existing alcove. The advantage of making your own cupboard is that you can tailor it to suit your needs – we chose a long, upward-hinging top section; two central doors; and two small drawers at the base.

If your existing cupboard is just too useful to part with, but too ugly to live with, why not give it a facelift by replacing the façade and doors, as explained in steps 1–8 overleaf?

MAKING THE BOX AND DRAWERS

1 The cupboard is assembled as a free-standing box. Begin by measuring the alcove to be filled, then subtract 7.5 cm (3 in) from the overall dimensions to ensure that the cupboard fits. Cut out the basic shapes with a hand saw; use a jigsaw for the curved side pieces. Smooth the cut edges with sandpaper.

2 Working on a flat surface, make up the basic box (cupboard), butting the sides into the top and base. First drill pilot holes for the screws through the top and base into the sides, then glue along all joining surfaces and reinforce with wood screws. You can now screw the back section onto the box. Use the exploded diagram (right) for guidance.

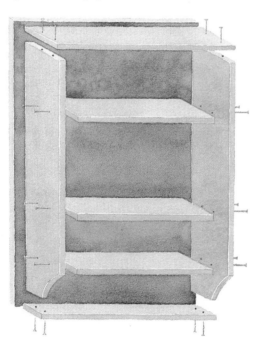

3 Mark the position of the shelves on the back of the box, using a spirit level to check they are straight. Drill pilot holes through from the sides and back, glue along joining surfaces and screw the shelves in place.

▼ TIP

If you measure your alcove accurately and take the plan to a timber merchant, they should be able to work out the exact quantities of wood that you need.

4 To ensure the drawers move freely inside the cupboard, fix four wooden battens to the bottom shelf with wood screws. Once again, you will have to drill pilot holes into the MDF before fixing the wooden battens in place.

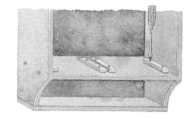

5 Measure the depth of the shelves and cut four drawer sides this length. Then measure the distance between the drawer runners, deduct 25 mm (1 in) from this length – this is the depth of the drawer sides – and cut out four lengths of MDF for the

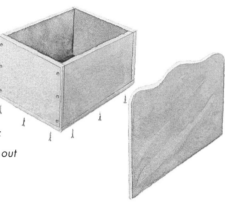

drawer fronts and backs.

To assemble the drawers, butt the front and back up against the sides, glue along all joining surfaces and secure with wood screws. Place the assembled box on top of the 6 mm (¼ in) MDF for the base, draw around the outline, then cut out the base. Glue in place on the bottom of the drawer and reinforce with screws up through the base.

6 Fix the assembled box securely to the back and side walls of the alcove using long steel masonry screws and wall plugs.

MAKING THE FRONT SECTION AND DRAWER HANDLES

TIP

If you are working with softwood or plywood, you can use a bradawl to make the pilot holes for the screws. If you are working with MDF, you will need to bore them with a drill.

1 Mark the shapes for the doors and drawers in pencil on the cupboard front. Make sure that you allow enough space between the cut-out shapes to provide a strong support frame, and enough at each side to fit the hinges. Make small pilot holes for the hinges with a drill or bradawl.

2 Support the cupboard front on a work bench with G-cramps, or raise it up on bricks. You need to allow enough clearance below the wood for the blade to move freely. Drill a small pilot hole into one of the marked lines, insert the blade and cut out the door and drawer shapes. Smooth the cut edges with fine sandpaper.

TIP

To minimize vibration, make sure you keep the jigsaw upright, with the base plate flat against the wood.

3 You can now fix the cupboard front to the assembled box. First make pilot holes down each side, then glue along all joining surfaces before fixing it in place with wood screws.

4 *If necessary, enlarge the fish and crocodile templates (see right) on a photocopier. Trace the outlines onto 12 mm (½ in) MDF and cut out the shapes with a jigsaw or coping saw. Smooth any rough edges with fine sandpaper.*

Cut the wooden dowel into four 20 mm (¾ in) lengths – these are used to support the handles on the drawers.

5 *You can now prime and paint the cupboard front. We used yellow for the front and different shades for the drawers and doors. Also prime and paint the three wooden door knobs and the fish and crocodile handles. Paint the wooden dowels the same colour as the drawers.*

6 *Glue the wooden cupboards onto the 'false' drawer fronts, then glue the 'false' drawer fronts onto the actual drawers. When the glue is dry, drill a pilot hole through the middle of each dowel into the drawer front. Then glue the painted animal handles in place on the wooden dowels.*

ABOVE: THE FISH AND CROCODILE TEMPLATE PATTERNS FOR THE HANDLES. DRAW THEIR OUTLINES ONTO MDF, THEN CUT OUT THE SHAPES USING AN ELECTRIC JIGSAW OR COPING SAW.

TIP

It is easy to customize an existing wardrobe by fixing new door and drawer handles. Why not design your own motifs to match the décor of the room?

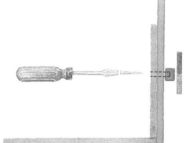

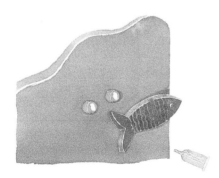

7 *To reinforce the drawer fronts, insert a screw through all four layers – drawer front, 'false' drawer front, wooden dowel and handle – from the inside. Screw the three painted door knobs on the cupboard doors.*

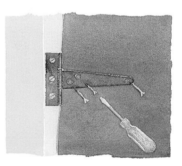

8 *Finally, locate the pilot holes for the hinges and screw the doors in position on the cupboard front.*

The biggest changes in this room were achieved by ruthlessly ripping out some badly designed fitted cupboards, pulling up a shag-pile carpet and having a lot of fun with paint. Once we had decided on the look – green and cream checks – we were able to use gingham fabric to pull the elements together.

The *Little* Girl's Room

BELOW: THE ROOM WAS A JUMBLE OF TOYS, SHELVING, CUPBOARDS AND BOXES – SET AGAINST A BACKDROP OF DATED PAINT EFFECTS.

BELOW: EVEN THOUGH WE USED A LOT OF
DIFFERENT SHADES AND PAINT FINISHES,
THE FINISHED ROOM LOOKS QUITE SIMPLE
AND HARMONIOUS. IN THE END, WE REALLY
FEEL WE HAVE ACHIEVED OUR OBJECTIVE
AND GIVEN THIS LITTLE GIRL THE PRETTIEST
ROOM IN WHICH TO GROW.

The first school years signal the start of an independent life for your child. You are still number one, but it is now the teacher who knows everything. Among your child's new friends, somebody else will have the best bedroom in the whole wide world, and these friends are described as so lucky. We have all been there and, unlike babyhood or snatched glimpses of nursery days, these are usually our first clear childhood memories. At this age, most brothers and sisters who have happily shared bedrooms in the past decide that they want rooms of their own. School teaches them that boys do some things and girls do others – and no amount of politically correct parenting can overcome this. The room we decorated for this age group looks undeniably feminine, but ideas like upholstering a stool, curtaining off a sink, colourwashing and painting checks on a wall, or simply painting the floor, can all be easily adapted to suit a typical boy's room. Just choose a different fabric, leave off the frills and don't show him these pictures!

DECORATIVE THEMES

Children mature at different ages, but six- or seven-year-olds can appear to drift between being much younger or far older than their actual age. One day they will announce that their old soft toys are far too babyish to be seen with, and the next they will shed bitter tears over the discovery that a younger visitor has wandered off with one of them. They want to grow up fast – but only when it

suits them. This changeability makes it difficult to decide on a decorating scheme, but this is a time to put the nursery years behind you and decorate you must.

Primary-age kids go through a lot of phases, and you may achieve near sainthood if you provide them with the very latest style and colour favoured by their pop star heroes and heroines. However, when their idols fall from grace, be prepared to redecorate. Part of growing up is to like things that your parents don't , and if you indulge their tastes too much you are in danger of spoiling their fun. Choose a look that is simple, but stylish enough to be the backdrop for all their primary years.

FURNITURE

Practical additions can be a dressing table or work top and a comfortable stool or chair, enough easily accessible storage to encourage tidiness, and a full-width single bed. If space is limited, consider buying a single unit that includes all of these things. There are many styles on the market that incorporate sleeping areas, storage and desk space (see page 74). Choose one that is made from solid timber, rather than coated fibreboard, because the extra cost is reflected in a far longer life expectancy. It is no good giving a boisterous child somewhere exciting to climb up and swing from, and then telling him or her not to do so because it will fall apart. Children of primary school age are still young enough to

LEFT: WE REPLACED THE TALL AND IMPRACTICAL FITTED CUPBOARD WITH THIS STYLISH CHILDREN'S WARDROBE, COMPLETE WITH TWO LARGE DRAWERS BELOW A REACHABLE HANGING RAIL. CHILDREN OF THIS AGE ENJOY ORGANIZING THEIR OWN SPACE, SO WE PROVIDED WICKER BASKETS AND A SET OF WOODEN BOXES. SOFT TOYS ARE STILL A PROMINENT FEATURE, AND IT IS A REAL BONUS TO BE ABLE TO PROP THEM UP AROUND THE SIDES OF THE BED.

want to make camps, play hide and seek and pretend they're abseiling down the side of a building to rescue their best friend.

Don't feel that you have to fill every inch of space. Instead, give your child room to move, dance and play. Supply at least one mirror to pose in front of – whether they aspire to be Gladiators or ballerinas, they will want to see what they look like. Let them choose pictures for the walls, and if you have a child who loves cutting pictures from magazines, then supply a large pinboard and preserve your paintwork. Think of the way schools line corridors with softboard to display children's work, and follow their example. The board can be

BELOW: THE BED WAS A MAIL-ORDER FIND, BOUGHT AS AN UNPAINTED FLAT PACK. WE PAINTED IT WITH TWO SHADES OF BLUE-GREEN EMULSION, LEAVING VISIBLE BRUSHSTROKES TO ADD INTEREST TO THE SMOOTHNESS OF THE MDF. THE STYLE IS A WONDERFUL COMBINATION OF THE SECURITY OF A LARGE COT AND THE ROMANCE OF A SCANDINAVIAN DAY BED.

fixed to the wall, then painted to match the rest of the room (see pages 64-5).

STORAGE

Make sure that you provide plenty of storage space: you will need a closet for hanging clothes, a place for folded clothes and somewhere to keep small items such as socks and underwear together. A second-hand, adult-size wardrobe can be adapted to be a lot more space-efficient. You won't need the full hanging length, so lower the rail to make room for a shelf above. This will still leave enough room below the hanging space for a set of plastic boxes to accommodate the smaller items. Bulky clothes like jumpers and tracksuits can go on the top shelf. See this redecorating time as an opportunity to ruthlessly edit your child's clothing and give away anything that is too small. Children grow so fast at this age that you may find you can halve their storage needs if you have a clear-out on a regular basis.

FLOORS

New floor coverings can be a major expense, but we kept the cost down in this room by painting the existing floorboards. We originally planned to strip the boards, but on finding that they weren't good enough we decided to save ourselves time and money by painting and varnishing them instead. Painted floors are ideal for kid's rooms, because spilled drinks, crushed chalks and other little mishaps can all be cleared up easily. Also, the paint seals

the wood which makes splinters less likely. We used three rag rugs as soft 'islands' in the heavy traffic areas.

WINDOWS

This room's large windows needed shading, but heavy curtains would have been very expensive. Instead, we used unlined muslin curtains in front of cream blackout blinds. These blinds are slightly more expensive than ordinary roller blinds because, although they look identical from the front, they have a special grey lining which completely blocks out daylight.

ABOVE: WE PAINTED AN OLD WOODEN BEDSIDE CUPBOARD TO MATCH THE ROOM'S DÉCOR AND FOUND A PRETTY LACE SHADE FOR THE OLD LAMP BASE. THE BED LOOKS REALLY INVITING PILED UP WITH ASSORTED CUSHIONS AND SOFT TOYS.

Sink curtains

A small corner sink already existed in this room, but the pipework beneath it made it look ugly and utilitarian – even though it was actually a very pretty shape. We decided to make it more a part of the room by fitting a green gingham skirt around the sides, which not only hides the pipework, but also provides a useful storage area for toiletries and cleaning products.

YOU WILL NEED... *Two 12 cm (5 in) lengths of wooden batten • An electric drill fitted with a 7 mm masonry bit • Masking tape • Brown wall plugs • Gauge 10 chipboard screws, 75 mm (3 in) long • A 12 cm (5 in) strip of hardboard • Panel pins • A hammer • furnishing fabric in your chosen colour • Sewing thread • Dressmaker's pins • 2.5 cm (1 in) curtain heading tape • Plain or self-adhesive Velcro tape*

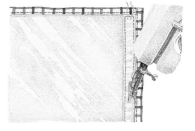

1 *The curtains are secured with Velcro to a piece of hardboard that fits around the sink. You will need to fix a short batten on either side of the sink to support the hardboard. First drill holes into the side walls, just below the sink, then insert rawlplugs. Fix the battens in place with chipboard screws.*

TIP

When drilling into tiles, place a small strip of masking tape on the wall to prevent the drill bit from slipping.

2 *Dampen the hardboard to make it more flexible, then attach it, shiny side out, under the sink. First fix one side to a batten, using a row of panel pins, then bend the hardboard into a curve and fix the other side to the batten on the opposite side.*

3 *Cut out the two curtain panels, making each one the same width as the hardboard to allow for the gathers. Cut out a 12 cm (5 in) frill for each curtain, making them twice the width of each curtain panel.*

4 *Neaten the raw edges of each curtain by turning under a narrow hem around all four sides. To gather the top edge, stitch a length of heading tape to the wrong side, catching in the cords down one side only.*

5 *The frills are made from single thickness fabric, which is hemmed around all four edges and gathered at the top. Start by stitching a narrow hem around all four sides, then gather the top edge with two parallel rows of stitching.*

LEFT: WE GAVE THE SINK A FEMININE LOOK WITH A FRILLED GINGHAM SKIRT. THE EXISTING TILES DIDN'T SUIT THE NEW DÉCOR, SO WE COATED THEM WITH WHITE SATINWOOD PAINT AND ADDED A BLUE BROKEN STRIPE IN ARTIST'S OIL PAINT.

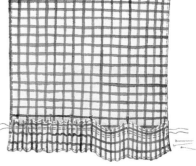

6 Lay the curtain panels right side up on a work surface and place a frill right side up along the lower edge of each. Pin the frill to the curtain at the centre and side edges, then pull up the gathering threads to fit. Pin, then topstitch in place.

7 We fixed our curtains to the hardboard with Velcro, but you could use staples and net curtain wire instead. Cut a piece of Velcro to fit, and fix the looped side to the hardboard. Pull up the cords on the curtain header tapes, then attach the other half of the Velcro over the top. Press the Velcro strips together to hang the curtains.

Wall treatment

These walls incorporate a hand-painted frieze above the picture rail that was inspired by the work of Carl Larsson. This Swedish painter and decorative artist lived an idyllic family life, which was reflected in the way he decorated the family home. The frieze of swags and ribbons that we have used around the top of this room is similar to one that he designed for his own children's shared bedroom. It is painted in acrylic glazes.

CREATING THE HAND-PAINTED FRIEZE

1 Start by making up the two acrylic glazes: the first contains one part Venetian Red acrylic paint, one part PVA glue and 2 parts water; the second consists of one part Raw Sienna acrylic paint, one part PVA glue and 2 parts water.

2 Using a soft pencil and a long ruler attached to a spirit level , mark a faint horizontal line 56 cm (22 in) below the coving. Use the 12 mm (½ in) square-tipped artist's brush to go over your marked outline freehand in Raw Sienna glaze.

Mark out vertical lines in pencil running from the horizontal line to the coving, at 75 cm (30 in) intervals. These are the ribbons. Then go over your outlines in red acrylic glaze, using the same square-tipped paintbrush.

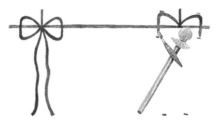

3 Paint a red bow and a tail on the end of each 'ribbon', using the the mahl stick to steady and control your brush. Rest the brush on the stick and lever it up, down and across. Each tail is slightly different – some twist, others curl – but they are all roughly the same length (30 cm/12 in).

4 To make a template for the swag, take a sheet of newspaper 75 cm (30 in) wide – this is the distance between the bows – and fold it in half.

5 Using the photograph as a guide, mark the curved outline of the swag on the newspaper and cut out the shape with scissors.

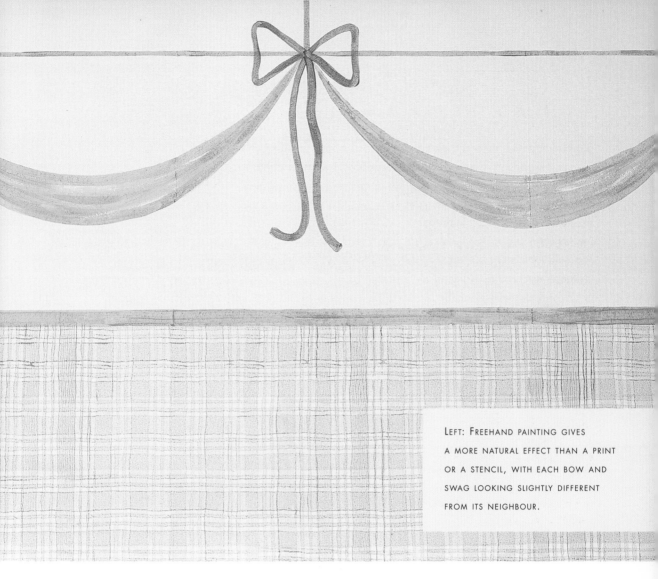

LEFT: FREEHAND PAINTING GIVES
A MORE NATURAL EFFECT THAN A PRINT
OR A STENCIL, WITH EACH BOW AND
SWAG LOOKING SLIGHTLY DIFFERENT
FROM ITS NEIGHBOUR.

6 Open out the paper template and position it between a pair of bows. Holding it steady with one hand, draw around the outline lightly in pencil.

7 Using the 10 mm (⅜ in) paintbrush, outline the swags with Raw Sienna glaze. Then fill in the middle with the same glaze to give a solid shape.

8 Finish by painting a 3 cm (1¼ in) horizontal stripe in Raw Sienna underneath the frieze, or use this colour to paint an existing picture rail.

TIP

Don't be tempted to squeeze the bows too close together. One of the characteristics of this border is the airy delicacy created by the space around the bows.

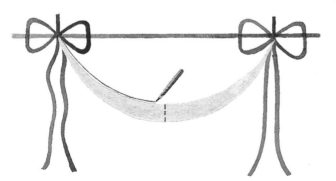

PAINTING THE PLAID WALL

Below the hand-painted frieze of swags and bows, we used one of our own effects – a plaid pattern produced by customizing a small sponge roller, then painting horizontal and vertical stripes.

The paint is diluted with PVA glue to make a gelatinous glaze that works particularly well when applied with a sponge roller. There is no need to protect the walls with varnish, since the glue acts as a sealant.

Below the dado rail, we applied two separate colourwashes in Venetian Red and Raw Sienna.

YOU WILL NEED...
A small sponge 'gloss' roller, 10 cm (4 in) wide • A felt-tip 'fine-liner' pen • A craft knife or scalpel • Acrylic paint in your chosen colour (we used Hookers Green) • PVA or white glue • A paint tray • A medium-sized household paintbrush

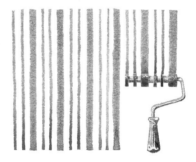

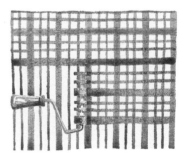

1 Mark the roller to show the spacing between the stripes. Using the felt-tip pen, draw bands around the foam then cut away the strips right down to the central tube with a craft knife to produce a relief pattern.

2 Make up the paint glaze. We used 1 part acrylic paint to 5 parts PVA glue and 3 parts water. Mix a generous amount and pour some of it into the paint tray.

3 Run the roller through the glaze until it is evenly coated. Beginning in the top left-hand corner (unless you are left-handed), start rolling down the wall from the picture rail. Apply even light pressure, but do not worry too much about variations in the strength of colour – that is the desired effect.

4 Once the verticals are dry, you can start painting the horizontal stripes. Again, begin in the top left-hand corner, but this time work across the room parallel with the picture rail. Once the horizontals are complete, use an ordinary paintbrush to fill in the corners with a solid stripe.

ABOVE: THE FINISHED EDGES OF BOTH OF THESE PAINT EFFECTS WERE QUITE RAGGED, SO WE DISGUISED THEM BY FITTING A DADO RAIL.

PAINTING THE COLOURWASHED WALL

1 Make up the two colour-washes using half acrylic paint and half PVA glue. Dilute with 3 parts water.
NOTE: Once the paint and glue are mixed together, the colour appears milky, but this will clear as the paint dries.

TIP

The PVA glue should prevent the colour from running. If drips do occur, simply pick them up on the brush and work them into the wall.

2 Starting at a side edge, brush on the first colour – in this case, Venetian Red – with random brushstrokes. Work quickly and vigorously. Leave to dry before applying the second colour.

YOU WILL NEED...
Artist's acrylic paints in your chosen colours (we used Venetian Red and Raw Sienna) • PVA or white glue • A large household paintbrush (it must be comfortable for you to hold) • A paint kettle

3 Apply the second colour-wash over the first in the same way and leave to dry.

BELOW: THIS SIMPLE DRESSING TABLE WAS CREATED FROM TWO PIECES OF PINE SHELVING AND FOUR STAIR BALUSTERS, WHICH WE BOUGHT FROM A DIY CHAIN. THE ADVANTAGE OF BUILDING YOUR OWN FURNITURE IS THAT YOU CAN MAKE IT TO YOUR OWN SPECIFICATIONS.

Dressing table stool

Upholstery is one of those tasks that is usually reserved for the professionals, or at least someone who has done a few evening classes. But even a complete novice, if armed with a staple gun, can reupholster a stool like this one. We decided to go for a co-ordinated look, and used the same green gingham as for the sink curtains.

ABOVE: WE GAVE THIS PIANO STOOL A NEW LEASE OF LIFE WITH A COAT OF CREAM PAINT AND NEW GINGHAM UPHOLSTERY.

YOU WILL NEED...
Furnishing fabric in your chosen colour • A pair of dressmaker's scissors • A staple gun • Ricrac braid to fit around the stool • Fabric adhesive • Dressmaker's pins

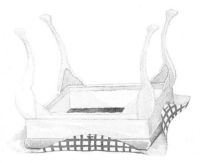

1 *Lay the fabric wrong side up on the floor and place the stool upside down on top. Roughly trim away any excess fabric around the sides.*

Staple the fabric to the edge of the stool on one side, inserting a single staple at the half-way point. Then pull the fabric taut on the opposite side and staple in place as before. Staple the fabric to the ends of the stool in the same way, then turn the stool the right way up.

2 *Working from the centre, staple outwards on each side. Staple the fabric around all four edges to within 2.5 cm (1 in) of the corners. Make sure you pull the fabric taut with your hand each time you insert a staple.*

To create a neat finish at the corners, pleat the fabric before you insert the staples. First trim away the corner point, then pleat evenly to fit the corner exactly. Staple in place before trimming away any excess fabric.

3 *Measure the circumference of the stool and make up a single thickness frill, following the method explained on page 48, step 5. As a general rule, the length of the frill should be twice the circumference of the stool. Gather the upper edge of the frill to fit the stool and staple in place.*

4 *To give a neat finish, cover the staples by gluing a length of braid around the stool. You may need to insert a few dressmaker's pins to hold the braid in place until the glue dries, but make sure that you remove these once the glue has bonded.*

This attic bedroom had not been properly decorated for years. It had simply been covered with hundreds of flyers, posters and beermats. As is often the case in attic rooms, it was furnished with cast-offs from the rest of the house and had a shambolic, teenage sitcom look.

The Teenager's Room

BELOW: THE SLOPING CEILING DOMINATED THE ROOM, WITH ITS RIOT OF COLOURFUL FLYERS THAT MADE THE ROOM LOOK SMALLER AND DARKER THAN IT ACTUALLY WAS.

Teenagers have a lot of decisions to make – they need to assert their independence and be territorial about their `own space'. Some teenagers will take this very literally and turn their rooms into no-go areas where standards of hygiene, tidiness, noise pollution and colour co-ordination are a very deliberate opposite to those you uphold in the rest of your home. Others are just too lazy to bother fighting the system and express no opinion whatsoever about plans to decorate their rooms. But not everyone conforms to these stereotypes – a lot of teenagers watch *Home Front,* judging by the mailbags filled with requests for make-overs, and

they recognize that personal style extends beyond the clothes you wear to the environment you choose to live in.

CHOOSING A THEME

Designer labels have a huge influence on young people and most teenagers are familiar with the look as well as the labels of fashion icons such as Ralph Lauren, Calvin Klein and Giorgio Armani. The clothes might be too expensive for a teenager's pocket, but there is a whole package of associated advertising that comes free in magazines and shops to reinforce the style. Today's teenagers are probably the first generation to have this level of design awareness, and it would be a shame if this meant good design was seen as just another sort of fashion craze, here today and gone tomorrow.

Collect fabric swatches and colour cards, and let them decide how they want the room to look – then involve them in budgeting! This way, they will understand any practical compromises that have to be made. And when the time for action comes, get them to help with the actual hands-on decorating. As parents, we so often decide that it is easier and less messy to do the work ourselves. But at this stage in their lives, it is more important for them to experience the decision-making process and the reality of hard work so that they understand the satisfaction that comes from a job well done.

Before you decide on colour and style, make a list of any practical necessities:

ABOVE: AN ALUMINIUM PEGGED HANGING RAIL DISPLAYS A COLLECTION OF FAVOURITE DESIGNER LABELS. THIS ONE WAS A CHAIN-STORE FIND AND HAS A USEFUL SHELF ABOVE THE PEGS.

BELOW: THE PERSONAL GROOMING SIDE OF THE ROOM HAS SHOES AND CLOTHING NEATLY ARRANGED, A PEG RAIL FOR ACCESSORIES, A LAUNDRY BASKET AND, MOST IMPORTANTLY, A MIRROR. THE MIRROR HAS USEFUL ALUMINIUM PEGS BELOW IT FOR HANGING A WASHBAG FULL OF GELS, MOUSSES, BRUSHES, COMBS AND OTHER HAIRSTYLING ESSENTIALS.

anything that can be re-vamped, and also the things that they are ready to edit from their childhoods. They should not be rushed into getting rid of things immediately – instead, provide a few strong cardboard cartons that can be filled and stored away in the attic to provide instant nostalgia in the future.

ORGANIZED LIVING

These are the homework years and you can help make these hours more bearable by providing a really sturdy, well-lit worktop with plenty of shelving and a comfortable chair. If they feel businesslike when they sit down to work, it will be a lot easier for them to get down to business. If you confine homework to one area, it is prevented from spreading out and devouring the rest of the room. They also need space for lounging about, listening to music, watching TV, playing electronic games, dancing, exercising and entertaining their friends. It sounds as if they need their own apartment and most would be inclined to agree!

STARTING FROM SCRATCH

This thirteen-year-old boy's room had been a riot of unmatching furniture, abandoned clothing and football and music memorabilia. The room seemed much smaller than it was because of the sloping ceiling, his much loved double bed inherited from a spare bedroom and a very old settee. We decided to go for a complete change and give him the very latest `industrial' look of bare metal combined with a background of camouflage green and pale coffee. He gave us permission to change everything – the only thing that we kept was his lampshade! The result was a very different and sophisticated look that he absolutely loved, and so did his friends.

We replaced his blind with wooden shutters and used the same matt green to paint an old pine single bed and the rest of the room's woodwork. The new carpet was a contractor's remnant and such a

bargain that we abandoned our original idea of using cork and rubber industrial flooring. Instead of the usual bedding, we made the bed into a daytime settee using three rolled-up sleeping bags as bolsters, which also provide instant beds when friends stay over. All of his clothes are contained in an open wardrobe unit, working on the idea that if it looks like a shop display he may want to keep it tidy. The fitted worktop houses all his schoolwork, as well as his TV, CD player and magazine collection. We made the door surround into a large pinboard for all his cuttings, notices and photographs.

We have to own up to providing one real luxury for this lucky boy in the

BELOW: THE CUSHIONS CAN BE INSTANTLY CONVERTED INTO A COMFORTABLE SPARE BED, WHICH IS JUST AS EASY TO PUT BACK IN ITS PLACE IN THE MORNING. THIS IS THE KIND OF LOW-MAINTENANCE STYLE THAT REALLY WORKS WITH TEENAGERS. THE ADJUSTABLE LAMP CAN BE TILTED DOWN FOR READING OR UPWARDS TO SPOTLIGHT HOMER SIMPSON.

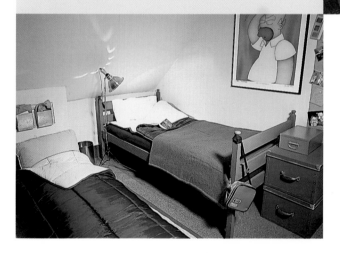

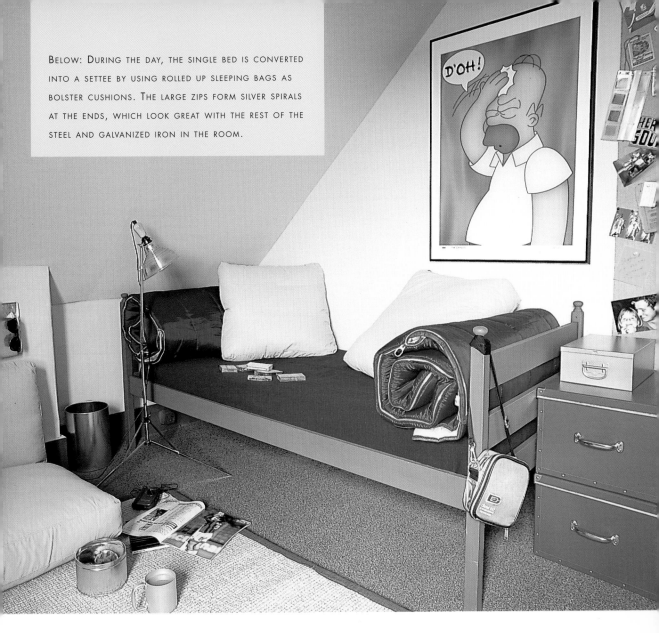

BELOW: DURING THE DAY, THE SINGLE BED IS CONVERTED INTO A SETTEE BY USING ROLLED UP SLEEPING BAGS AS BOLSTER CUSHIONS. THE LARGE ZIPS FORM SILVER SPIRALS AT THE ENDS, WHICH LOOK GREAT WITH THE REST OF THE STEEL AND GALVANIZED IRON IN THE ROOM.

shape of a small black fridge filled with his favourite canned soft drinks. Imagine being a teenager with a fridge in your bedroom – cool, or what? To do this on the cheap, look out for a second-hand bedsit fridge and let your teenager rejuvenate it with a fresh coat of matt black spray paint.

The room was designed to appeal to teenagers of both sexes and the same style could be given a much more feminine look just by using a different colour scheme. Imagine spicy red woodwork with mustard yellow walls or chalky lavender pink walls with sky blue woodwork. Experiment together by cutting up colour charts from paint manufacturers and putting unusual combinations of colours next to each other. Take a walk on the wild side and you may even be inspired to redecorate your own bedroom next.

Window shutters

Proper internal shutters are extremely expensive to buy and fit, so instead we decided to use standard louvre doors that are sold by DIY outlets. As all windows are different sizes, we cannot specify which louvre doors to buy. Instead, we show you how to adapt slightly larger louvres to fit. We felt that four shutters worked best on this Victorian sash window – they also enable you to create a stylish half-shuttered window effect.

> YOU WILL NEED... *A tape measure • 2 or 4 louvre doors • 5 x 2.5 cm (2 x 1 in) timber batten, the same height as your window frame • A hand saw • An electric drill fitted with a 7 mm masonry bit • Gauge 10 chipboard screws, 75 mm (3 in) long • Brown wall plugs • A screwdriver • A pencil • A spirit level • Green chalkboard paint or eggshell in your chosen colour • A small foam roller or household paintbrush • 4 or 8 brass butt hinges, 5 cm (2 in) long • A bradawl*

1 *The shutters must be fitted flush onto the window frame, so that they present a flat front and also fold back onto the wall if there is space. Start by measuring your existing window frame, bearing in mind that you will need to fix a flat strip of timber batten down each side to take the hinges. The shutters should be bought larger than the frame, not smaller, if you cannot get a perfect fit.*

TIP

Make an easy job of painting the louvres by leaning them against a wall at an angle. Use a small foam roller in one hand to paint the accessible flat surfaces and a paintbrush in the other to pick up runs and fill in gaps.

2 *Assuming that the shutters are wider than the window frame, cut two lengths of batten and fix them to the wall on either side of the frame – check the position of each by holding two shutters over the window and marking the edges with a pencil. Check the verticals with a spirit level and screw the battens into the wall.*

3 *Paint the shutters, using a roller and paintbrush. Also paint the frame and the battens.*

4 Fit two brass hinges to the underside of each shutter, then hold them up against the window to mark the screw positions on the batten or frame. You will need a helper to check that the shutters are vertical, and to ensure that they open and close smoothly. If you are fitting four shutters, you should fit the top set first.

ABOVE: THE SHUTTERS LOOK GOOD WHETHER OPEN OR CLOSED. A PAIR OF THEM ON EACH SIDE LEAVES THE OPTION OF JUST CLOSING THE LOWER HALF FOR PRIVACY AT NIGHT, WHILE LEAVING THE TOP HALF OPEN TO LET IN DAYLIGHT IN THE MORNING. (WE ADMIT THAT THE WELL-STOCKED FRIDGE IS A LUXURY – BUT, HEY, THE KITCHEN IS MILES AWAY!)

Pinboard

A doorway is the ideal place to site a pinboard, as it will always catch your attention on your way out. The size of the pinboard depends on the amount of information you want to display – whether it's timetables and postcards or posters and flyers. If you have lots of material, you may even decide to cover an entire wall with softboard.

RIGHT: THE GREEN DOOR IS SURROUNDED BY MEMENTOES, REMINDERS AND FAVOURITE PHOTOGRAPHS. WE HAVE PROVIDED PLENTY OF PEGS ELSEWHERE IN THE ROOM IN THE HOPE THAT THE DOOR WILL STAY COAT-FREE. THE BAG CONTAINS THINGS THAT NEED TO BE REMEMBERED FOR SCHOOL.

YOU WILL NEED... *A tape measure • Softboard to fit your chosen area • A pencil • A try square • A heavy-duty craft knife • A straight metal edge to cut along • An electric drill fitted with a 7 mm masonry bit • Brown wall plugs • Mirror fixings (these screws sink into washer surrounds to spread the stress load) • A screwdriver*

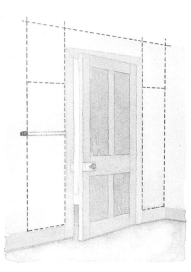

1 Measure the space around the door. This door has limited space on one side and above, so to give a balanced feel we decided to use the same width softboard on either side of the door.

2 Place the board on a flat surface and measure then mark the shapes to be cut. Use a try square to check that the angles are 90 degrees.

3 Using a sharp, heavy-duty craft knife or scalpel along a straight metal edge, cut out the shapes. Aim for as clean an edge as possible.

4 Mark out the position of the screws on the wall and drill then plug the holes. The softboard is extremely lightweight, so you will not need many screw holes. Attach the softboard to the wall with mirror fixings (see above).

Worktop

Many attic bedrooms have part-sloped ceilings, making it difficult to find furniture to fit. This desk is designed to make the most of the available space. The storage unit, which is made from MDF or plywood, can be customized to store all manner of equipment – from TV and computer to CDs and books.

ABOVE: WITH SO MUCH WELL PLANNED STORAGE ON AND AROUND THE DESK, EVEN A TEENAGER WOULD FIND IT HARD TO MAKE A MESS HERE. OK, QUITE HARD. ANYWAY, THERE'S A PLACE FOR EVERYTHING AND IT ALL LOOKS SO GOOD WHEN IT'S TIDY THAT THERE'S. A REAL INCENTIVE TO KEEP IT THAT WAY.

1 Having decided on the length and depth of the worktop, measure the space and cut the timber to fit.

2 Build the framework for the worktop. Start by fixing a strip of batten along the back wall, then fix another strip to the side wall. Use a spirit level to check the horizontals.

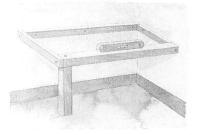

3 Cut the leg support to the correct height and ask someone to hold it in place. Rest the 2.5 x 2.5 cm (1 x 1 in) battening on top, using a spirit level to check that it is horizontal, then fix to the wall frame. First drill a pilot hole through from the front, then fix in place with screws. Connect the rest of the supporting frame by attaching the outside batten to the leg support.

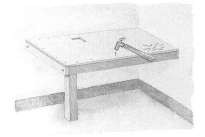

4 Cut a piece of MDF to fit the top. If desired, use a keyhole saw or jigsaw to cut a channel in the top to take any electrical wires. Rest the MDF on the batten framework and fix in place with panel pins.

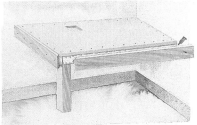

5 To neaten the side and front edges, fit two fascia strips around the outer edges of the worktop. You will need to mitre the fascia strips at the corner using a mitre-block. Glue the strips in place, then reinforce with panel pins from the outside.

6 Prepare the wood for painting by sanding the fascia strips, paying particular attention to the corner. Prime and paint the sides and support leg with chalkboard or eggshell paint in your chosen colour.

YOU WILL NEED...

5 x 2.5 cm (2 x 1 in) batten for the back and sides of the frame • A tape measure • A hand saw • A spirit level • An electric drill fitted with a 7 mm masonry bit • Rawl-plugs • Gauge 10 masonry screws, 75 mm (3 in) long • Chipboard screws, 38 mm (1½ in) long • A screwdriver • 7 cm (2¾ in) square post to support the corner of the frame • 2.5 x 2.5 cm (1 x 1 in) timber for the front of the frame • a sheet of 12 mm (½ in) MDF for the worktop • A keyhole saw or jigsaw (optional) • Panel pins • A small hammer • 7.5 x 2.5 cm (3 x 1 in) fascia strips • A mitre-block • Wood adhesive • Fine sandpaper • Masking tape • Wood primer • A small household paintbrush • Chalk-board or eggshell paint in your chosen colour

RIGHT: THIS MODULAR CLOTHING STORAGE UNIT CAN BE BOUGHT AS A CHROME FRAME AND FITTED WITH YOUR PERSONAL CHOICE OF HANGING COMPARTMENTS. ORIGINALLY RARE AND EXPENSIVE, THESE CAN NOW BE BOUGHT FROM MOST FURNITURE OUTLETS AND ALSO BY MAIL ORDER.

Other Storage

Keep a look out for shops that are closing down and snap up any chrome clothes rails that are going cheap. Second-hand office equipment suppliers have lots of interesting items like small metal filing cabinets that look fantastic when sand-blasted down to a bare metal finish, or metal filing trays and wire baskets. A worktop can be made from cheap fibreboard and given a metallic finish with silver aluminium paint. Edges can be faced with either a timber moulding or a chrome strip bought from a car accessory shop. Use kitchen basket trays on castors to slide underneath.

Old tin suitcases or canvas-covered cabin trunks make very stylish storage containers, especially if you are lucky enough to find a set in graduating sizes. Clean lines and plain shapes look best in industrial-style rooms, so keep to simple designs, avoid patterns and stick to a limited colour palette.

TIP

A very fashionable new twist to the bare metal look is sand-blasting, which involves the removal of paint with a high pressure blast of fine sand. Any metal box or cupboard of a reasonable thickness can be sand-blasted. It is not an expensive process, but you will have to take the items along to a workshop.

RIGHT: WE CHOSE THREE SEPARATE UNITS TO GO UNDER THE WORKTOP — ALL WITH THE SAME BARE METAL FINISH. CASTORS MEAN THAT THEY ARE EASY TO PULL OUT WHEN NEEDED. BASKETS ON WHEELS CAN BE USED FOR STORING ALL MANNER OF OBJECTS — FROM SOCKS AND BELTS TO SCHOOL-RELATED THINGS. THE DRAWER UNIT HOLDS SMALL ACCESSORIES SUCH AS PENS, PAPER CLIPS AND RULERS.

BEDS 72

FLOORS 76

WALLS 78

WINDOWS 80

STORAGE 82

LIGHTING 86

WORK SURFACES 88

SAFETY 90

The *Essentials*

One of the best things about decorating for children is that you have a relatively short time span in which to make decisions and get the job done. If you put it off now, your child will grow and its needs will change – so seize the moment and enjoy it. In this section of the book, we address basic issues such as which type of floor covering to go for; the best bed to choose; where to store things and how to create an exciting but safe environment for your child to grow in.

Beds

Cradles, like babies' shoes, hold a very special appeal, which probably comes from them being not strictly necessary – they just look so diminutive and adorable. Cots, on the other hand, are essential and it is no coincidence that they have bars resembling those on a wild animal's cage! Once your child is old enough to wander at will, the cot is replaced by a proper bed and this is one of the great milestones in a child's life.

Many mothers prefer to have their baby sleeping close by in the early weeks and a small cradle or a Moses basket can be placed alongside the bed at night within easy reach. Moses baskets have come a long way since the

ABOVE: A PRETTY WOODEN CRADLE IS SOON OUTGROWN AND IS NOT STRICTLY NECESSARY, BUT THE MATCHED PROPORTIONS OF BABY TO BED ARE AN ADORABLE SIGHT.

bulrush days and they can now be bought with all sorts of pretty, washable padded linings. Cribs and Moses baskets are the sorts of things that don't get worn out, so they are always available to buy second-hand. While this is a practical idea, bear in mind that health advice suggests you always buy a brand new mattress for a new baby – a small expense to bring peace of mind.

CRIB OR COT?

As to whether a crib should rock or not rock, the jury is still out – some point out that rocking is the most soothing and natural motion to calm a baby because it imitates life in the womb. Others will remind you that once you reintroduce rocking you are stuck with it. The truth is that all babies are different and maybe the ones that were rocked would have slept well anyway.

Many parents decide not to bother with a crib and manage very well with a full-sized cot from the outset. If this is your choice, make sure you place the baby 'foot to foot' – that is, with his feet touching one end of the cot. This way, the baby cannot shuffle down under the covers and overheat.

Cots are the sort of thing that are often put away in the attic for the next generation, and you may be offered one of these. Check it over carefully before accepting. Today's cots must conform to

LEFT: IF SPACE IS LIMITED
AND YOUR CHILD IS OLD
ENOUGH TO NEGOTIATE A
LADDER AT NIGHT, THEN
AN ARRANGEMENT LIKE
THIS ONE WILL DOUBLE THE
AMOUNT OF AVAILABLE
FLOORSPACE IN THE ROOM.
A HIGH PLATFORM WITH
CURTAINS MAKES A DEN
WITHIN THE ROOM.

high safety standards to prevent heads, hands and other bits from getting stuck. They must also have been painted with non-toxic paint or varnish. Pre-1960s cots, on the other hand, may have been coated with paint containing lead, which has been proved to be especially dangerous to children. As teething babies are likely to gnaw their cot bars, the health advice is not simply to repaint. Instead, you should have the cot paint-stripped professionally, and then you can re-coat it with modern, child-safe paint.

A baby will need a cot for the first two years of his life and some enjoy the

RIGHT: CHILDREN DON'T
NEED FULL-SIZED SINGLE
BEDS UNTIL THEY ARE
EIGHT OR NINE YEARS
OLD. IF YOU DECIDE TO
BUY A SMALL BED TO
BRIDGE THE GAP
BETWEEN COT AND BIG
BED, CHOOSE AN
INEXPENSIVE ONE LIKE
THIS MADE FROM MDF,
WHICH CAN BE PAINTED
TO MATCH YOUR
DECORATING SCHEME.

security so much that they are reluctant to give it up. One way of getting around this is to buy a cot-bed with removable sides. These are usually larger, more sturdy and more expensive than conventional cots, but they are a good investment that will last an average-sized child up to the age of four or five.

BED OR BUNK?

When you reach the 'big bed' stage, there are lots of exciting options. Cabin beds are good space-savers and they come in many combinations of single or double bunks with desk, play and storage space below. One company even makes a top bunk with a slide attachment for whizzing out of bed in the morning. The ideal age for this type of bed is from five upwards, when you feel that your child can sleep safely on a higher level and manage the ladder during the night. If you decide to keep to ground level, there are lots of different styles of bed. Most are full-length, but narrower than the normal single bed.

Novelty beds are not usually large enough to accommodate an older child, so at around the age of ten a good-quality single bed with a sprung mattress is a sound investment that will last through the teenage years. At this stage, you are no longer confined to the children's department.

ABOVE: CLEVER USE OF COVING AND MOULDINGS MAKES THESE BUNK BEDS LOOK LIKE PART OF THE BUILDING. EACH CHILD HAS AN ALCOVE WITH SHELVES FOR THEIR TREASURES AT THE FOOT OF THE BED. THE UNIT HAS BEEN DESIGNED WITH GREAT ATTENTION TO DETAIL, AS CAN BE SEEN ON THE HAND GRIP EXTENSION FOR THE LADDER.

RIGHT: THIS LITTLE BED GROWS WITH YOUR CHILD: IT CAN EXPAND THEN SHRINK FOR THE NEXT SMALL OCCUPANT.

ABOVE: POLISHED FLOORBOARDS ARE A PRACTICAL
OPTION FOR CHILDREN'S ROOMS BECAUSE THEY ARE
SO EASY TO KEEP CLEAN. A RUG LIKE THIS
HOPSCOTCH DESIGN WILL PROVIDE HOURS OF FUN
AND A SOFT PLAY SURFACE FOR OTHER GAMES.

Floors

Children spend much more time on the floor than adults, and their ages, characters and interests will provide the best clues to which type of flooring to choose. Bear in mind that it is easier for everyone if their floor covering is easy to clean, so make this a priority, together with comfort, good looks, noise reduction and affordability.

The first decision is whether to fit carpet or another type of flooring. A good-quality carpet provides unbeatable warmth and comfort, and it can be treated with a special chemical coating to guard against stains. If you are on a tight budget, search out a local firm that handles commercial contract carpeting, as they often have off-cuts and roll-ends large enough to do a child's bedroom.

If the room is large, consider carpeting just half of it. You can then create a soft area for walking barefoot and lazing about, and a smooth vinyl or cork surface where toy cars and dolls' prams can get up speed and snacks can be dropped with impunity.

Vinyl tiles are extremely practical and come in many brilliant matt colours that can be used to make bold chequerboards, which are great fun to live with. On the downside, its practicality gives it 'school' overtones and a bedroom should feel more personal and cosy than that.

Cork tiles can be bought varnished or plain from DIY stores and should be laid onto a level surface. The plain tiles can be laid in their natural colour or tinted with brilliant wood stains and arranged

RIGHT: A STENCILLED FLOOR LIKE THIS ONE
TAKES SOME PLANNING, BUT WILL GIVE YOU
A TREMENDOUS SENSE OF ACHIEVEMENT

BELOW: CUSHIONED VINYL FLOORING IS
SOFT TO WALK ON, NON-ALLERGENIC AND
EASY TO KEEP HYGIENICALLY CLEAN.

in borders or as a chequerboard. The
surface has a slight springiness that
children of all ages like, and cork is also
effective for noise reduction. Sealed cork
floors behave like vinyl and can be wiped
clean; they also make a sympathetic
background for rugs and dhurries.

If you are thinking long term, go for a
practical easy-clean surface in the early
years and plan to fit a good-quality
carpet when your youngster can be
introduced to the pleasures of vacuuming.

ABOVE: VINYL IS IMMENSELY PRACTICAL
FOR CHILDREN'S ROOMS AND COMES
IN ALL SORTS OF SUITABLE PATTERNS
AND COLOURS.

Walls

Decorating the walls of our houses can be a daunting business. All too often we play it safe and rely upon accessories to make our style statements for us. This all changes when we have the chance to decorate for children. We are seized by their sense of fun and love of colour – and there are so many colours to choose from.

If you are decorating for a young child, your best bet is a wipe-clean surface so that spilt drinks or scribbles can be removed with minimum fuss. If you go for painted walls, choose a vinyl silk emulsion, or coat ordinary emulsion paint with clear matt varnish. Your choice of decorating styles is virtually limitless. Simple shapes like stars, suns, spots or numerals can look stunning as a border or an all-over pattern, and these effects are easy to achieve yourself with either pre-cut or home-made stencils.

THEMES AND STYLES

Most older children have passionate interests and may want their rooms decorated to reflect them. Themes could include a football club, a comic book hero or an obsession with horses. There is no denying that you will be a popular parent if you indulge them, but you should weigh up the pros and cons beforehand – if they support a particular football team, offer to decorate the walls in the team colours without actually using club wallpaper. Or try and get away with painting the floor green with white lines to imitate a pitch.

By the time your child reaches the teenage years, style becomes an important issue. If you can find the generosity in your heart to let them decide on a particular wall treatment, it will make your life easier. On a practical level, provide masses of display space by covering one or two walls with soft board, which can be painted to match the rest of the room. And remember – whichever colour they choose, paint is a wonderful substance and even black will disappear under a few coats of white!

BELOW: CREATE A CORNER OF THE JUNGLE WITH A LEAFY MURAL PAINTING AND BY HANGING MASKS AND EXOTIC BIRDS FOR A THREE-DIMENSIONAL EFFECT.

ABOVE: IF YOU ARE PAINTING AN ALL-OVER PATTERN OR MURAL, DON'T FEEL THAT IT HAS TO STOP AT THE RADIATOR. TREAT IT AS JUST ANOTHER SURFACE AND DISGUISE ITS SHAPE BY PAINTING YOUR DESIGN OVER IT, AS HAS BEEN DONE WITH THIS HUMPTY-DUMPTY MURAL.

ABOVE: YOU CAN HAVE LOTS OF FUN DECORATING A CHILD'S ROOM. THE BOLD WALLPAPER WITH ITS ROSY SPOTS DROPS RIGHT BACK ALONGSIDE THE LARGE WHITE DOTS THAT HAVE BEEN SPONGED ONTO THE FIREPLACE AND SKIRTING BOARD.

RIGHT: BIG STENCILS ARE GREAT FOR QUICK TRANSFORMATIONS. CHOOSE SIMPLE SHAPES LIKE THIS DAISY AND DOT AND APPLY THEM RANDOMLY, JUDGING THE SPACING BY EYE. IN THIS ROOM THE DAISY PATTERN WAS ALSO CUT OUT OF THE BED SURROUND USING A JIGSAW, THEN THE SAME COLOURS WERE USED FOR THE BED AND THE FLOWER CENTRES.

Windows

Curtains or blinds are your two main choices when deciding how to treat the windows in your child's room. Much will depend upon the size and aspect of the windows. Curtains can make a room feel cosier in winter because they absorb draughts and noise, but good curtains use a lot of fabric and can be expensive to make. Blinds come in a variety of styles, ranging from flouncy to minimal, and tend to use less fabric.

In the early months, most babies sleep quite happily in broad daylight. However, as they become more aware, they find it difficult to settle unless the room is artificially darkened. Curtains should be fitted with a good lining fabric

to cut out light or used in conjunction with blackout roller blinds. These are more expensive than ordinary blinds, but are very effective.

QUICK CURTAINS

Sewing is no longer as popular as it used to be and consequently many of you will be buying ready-made curtains rather than making your own. Although the ready-made ranges used to be quite limited, they can now be bought in every kind of style, pattern and size. Many suppliers sell matching bedding too, if you want to go for a co-ordinated look. If you do decide to make your own curtains, this can be done in the

LEFT: MAKE THE MOST OF THE EXTRA SPACE CREATED BY A BAY WINDOW BY BUILDING IN A WINDOW SEAT WITH A HINGED LID THAT DOUBLES AS A TOY BOX. BY USING THE SAME FABRIC FOR THE BLIND, THE CURTAIN AND THE WINDOW SEAT CUSHION THE SPACE IS MADE TO LOOK DEEPER THAN IT REALLY IS. THE TEMPTATION TO CURL UP IN THERE WITH A BOOK AND THOSE CUDDLY TOYS ON A RAINY DAY WOULD BE IMPOSSIBLE TO RESIST.

conventional way or without sewing a stitch – all you need is an iron to heat-seal the special header and hemming tapes. Another time- and effort-saving idea is to use a curtain rod with clipped rings, which will hang most light- to medium-weight fabrics. These are particularly suitable for draping muslin, which can be bought in a good range of colours and patterns.

NO-SEW OPTIONS

If you go for blinds, there are lots of different types to choose from: bamboo, cane or paper are perfect for a natural look; Roman blinds, which operate on a system of concealed rods and strings, look stylish and make economical use of fabric; slatted blinds, which look like narrow Venetian blinds, provide a cool, modern, no-frills look; and Austrian blinds will transform any bedroom into a boudoir and make your daughter feel like a princess.

For an older child or teenager, try a more experimental approach. You can achieve stunning results by abandoning conventional curtain and blind fittings altogether and using a staple gun instead. Curtaining can be made to look simple and chic with regular pleating, or theatrical and 'over the top' with pelmets, swags and drapes. Stapling is best done using cheap rolls of market fabrics such as calico, muslin, suit lining, felt or mattress ticking – all of which can be ripped down and thrown away after a few years, because washing then rehanging is not really an option.

ABOVE: MATCHING CURTAIN TIE-BACKS ARE ONE OF THOSE FINISHING TOUCHES THAT TAKE VERY LITTLE TIME TO PUT TOGETHER BUT MAKE A HUGE DIFFERENCE.

LEFT: THE MAD HATTER TIE-BACKS HERE ARE ENLARGEMENTS OF A DESIGN ON THE CURTAIN FABRIC. THEY WERE CUT OUT OF MDF USING A JIGSAW THEN FIXED TO THE WALL ON A BRACKET. CHOOSE ANY FAVOURITE CHARACTER, ANIMAL OR VEHICLE AND GIVE IT THE SAME TREATMENT.

Storage

This has to be one of the most important considerations when designing and decorating a room for your child. There is little point making the room look great, if it is impossible to keep it that way. And to do that, you need a workable storage system. This applies equally whether you are doing up a box room for a newborn or an attic for a teenager – unless things are as easy to put away as they are to get out, the result will be a mess.

The size and shape of the room will have the most influence upon the route you take. A plain, featureless room offers a chance for you to start from scratch with your own ideas. In a room with a chimney breast, however, the obvious siting for cupboards is in the recesses on either side, so that you don't intrude into the main floor space. Many older houses have existing built-in cupboards, although the internal arrangements may not suit your needs. Think twice before ripping them out altogether. Instead, consider fitting new shelving and rails that make more efficient use of the space. Provide low hanging rails for short clothing and high shelves for out-of-season clothes and equipment.

SORT IT

If you want the neatness of closed cupboards without the hard work, simply build shelves into an alcove and hinge a pair of doors onto a simple batten frame. Clothing or toys can be sorted into transparent plastic boxes for easy access and identification (see page 31).

You can now buy sets of storage boxes in corrugated cardboard, jelly-coloured plastic, aluminium, framed

ABOVE: AN ALCOVE BESIDE A FIREPLACE CAN HOUSE A FREESTANDING WARDROBE LIKE THIS JUNK SHOP BARGAIN, REJUVENATED WITH A COAT OF PAINT.

LEFT: THRIFTY DECORATORS USED TO COVER GROCERY BOXES BUT NOW MATCHING SETS OF COLOURED CARDBOARD CARTONS ARE PRICED SO REASONABLY THAT THEY CAN BE THROWN OUT ONCE THEY LOOK TATTY. IDENTIFY BOXES WITH CUT-OUT PICTURES AND STICKERS TO ENCOURAGE CHILDREN TO KEEP TOYS TIDY.

BELOW: MAKE HANGING COATS UP A LOT MORE FUN BY PROVIDING A CHARACTER PEG RAIL, FIXED AT CHILD-HEIGHT.

canvas or woven willow. There are big or small boxes on wheels, boxes that fold flat and boxes that slide under beds. Storage is a big business and it now rates its own section in many large DIY, furniture and mail-order outlets. There are even specialist stores, whose entire focus is on the efficient stashing away of anything and everything we own. The problem is that if we were to put everything away as they suggest, our rooms would all look the same – exactly like the shops! We advise a bit of pick-and-mix – it makes life and shopping more interesting.

Children's needs change over the years, so try to make your storage as adaptable as possible. A baby might not be able to fish things out of cupboards, but a toddler will. At the toddler stage, you need to store things away out of their reach, making high cupboards and shelves invaluable. However, toddlers must also learn to make decisions in order to develop a sense of responsibility – whether it's choosing their own toys and activities or picking their favourite

LEFT: HANG-UP TIDY RAILS ENABLE YOU TO CHOOSE THE IDEAL COMBINATION OF COMPARTMENTS FOR YOUR POSSESSIONS. THESE PRACTICAL RAILS HAVE EVOLVED INTO STYLE STATEMENTS THAT COME IN A RANGE OF BRILLIANT COLOURS LIKE THIS, OR THE MINIMALIST'S FAVOURITE - UNBLEACHED CALICO. THIS RAIL FEATURES A USEFUL DOUBLE BAR ALONG THE BOTTOM THAT CAN BE USED AS A SHOE RACK OR TO HOUSE ROWS OF BOXES.

ABOVE: COAT HANGERS NEEDN'T BE DULL. CUT SOME LIKE THIS OUT OF PLYWOOD, THEN DECORATE.

things to wear. What they require is a selection of all these things within their reach as well. You cannot expect them to do all the clearing up, but if you start small with a couple of boxes, the idea of being tidy may catch on.

During the primary school years, children acquire puzzles, construction kits, games, technology and art materials at an alarming rate. A good shelving system with separate boxes for all their various activities will help them make the most of their playtime. You should also provide a large folder for their artworks. Young artistic efforts will be encouraged if you invest in boxes with compartments where art materials can be stored in separate groups of pens, crayons,

RIGHT: UNDERBED STORAGE CONTAINERS
SHOULD BE LIGHT ENOUGH TO SLIDE EASILY IN
AND OUT. THIS FOLDING PLASTIC BOX ON
WHEELS FITS NEATLY UNDER A CHILD'S BED.

BELOW: TIDINESS, EVEN FOR TEENAGERS, IS
ACHIEVABLE IF YOU HAVE AN WELL-PLANNED
STORAGE SYSTEM LIKE THIS.

mirror on the wall, remember to fit a shelf nearby to hold all those hair essentials, and put a CD or tape rack alongside the player.

Try providing an orderly storage system for their school books and equipment. It may make them feel more inclined to study if their schoolwork is confined to one part of the room.

And don't despair if you are not a shining example of tidiness – sometimes this can prove the greatest encouragement of all because, as we know, teenagers thrive on being different from their parents.

pencils and paint brushes. In the same way, a construction kit is easier to use if all the components are sorted into compartments. Buy a box made for the DIY market and help your child with the initial sorting out.

During the teenage years, toys are replaced by books, magazines, music, clothes and make-up. Now your child will need shelving for an entirely different set of possessions. At this age, clothes can be seen as a part of the décor, and a much-loved jacket, pair of trainers or dress is not something to hide away in a wardrobe. A chrome hanging rail with open canvas shelves may prove a more popular option, while a row of pegs on a rail is the ideal place to keep belts, scarves and jewellery. If you put a

LEFT: IF YOU CAN SPARE
JUST 60 CM (2 FT)
ALONG ONE SIDE OF THE
ROOM, SOLVE ALL YOUR
STORAGE PROBLEMS AT A
STROKE BY FITTING THE
WHOLE WALL WITH
SHELVES, RAILS AND
COMPARTMENTS. THE
SHELVES CAN BE BUILT
FROM MDF AND PAINTED.

Lighting

The way a room is lit is almost as important as the way it is decorated. There is little point using subtle colour combinations if you don't consider the lighting carefully. In children's rooms, looks are only part of the story. We also have to examine their specific needs. A worktop, for example, will be redundant without a light to work by; a pretty table lamp won't help them find their clothes; and a mirror is useless if they cannot get close enough to see themselves.

LIGHT EFFECTS

When we decorate a room, most of us either do so in daylight or under the full glare of artificial light. If you take time to consider the way the finished room is to be lit at an early stage, there are many more options.

All the wiring for wall lights, central or table lights will be much neater and safer if it is installed first and concealed as you decorate. It is possible to judge the effect of different kinds of lighting using torches or an inspection lamp to shine light up and down walls or to spotlight certain areas. This way, you will be in control of the room's lighting rather than having it determined by the proximity of a plug or an existing light fitting.

If there is to be just one lighting alteration in a child's room, it should be the fitting of a dimmer switch. Variable light is a real boon, whatever the child's

age. Turned down to its lowest strength, a dimmer switch will give enough light to comfort a child who is afraid of the dark; at a quarter strength, it will make the room look warm on a dull day; at half strength, it will provide enough light in the evening in conjunction with other task lighting; and on full strength, it makes an excellent searchlight!

Safety is paramount, so make sure that all plugs, sockets, switches and

ABOVE: FINDING THE RIGHT LAMPSHADE CAN BECOME A QUEST IN ITSELF, SO TRY MAKING YOUR OWN OR CUSTOMIZE A BOUGHT ONE BY ATTACHING DECORATIONS LIKE THESE.

ABOVE: CHOOSE BROAD-BASED BEDSIDE LAMPS FOR STABILITY. CHECK OUT CRAFT STORES AND FAIRS FOR BRIGHT, UNUSUAL DESIGNS.

BELOW: WALL LIGHTS ARE THE SAFEST OPTION IN A YOUNG CHILD'S ROOM. THIS MOON LIGHT CAN BE SCREWED TO THE WALL ANYWHERE WITHIN REACH OF A SOCKET.

cables are in perfect condition and don't have any trailing wires that could be tripped over. When choosing a bedside light for a young child, pick one with a very sturdy base or go for one that can be clipped onto a shelf or bed frame. Sockets that are not being used should be fitted with special socket covers or nursery night light plugs, which provide minimal light and seal sockets at the same time.

For the older child, an angle-poise lamp is a must for lighting a desk or worktop, while small clip-on spotlights are useful for reading and music areas. Check out the home departments in chain stores as well as the large DIY outlets because they all stock a good selection of contemporary light fittings that will appeal to design-conscious kids.

ABOVE: THE SOFT GLOW OF A NIGHT LIGHT IS VERY REASSURING. THESE LOW-VOLTAGE APPLIANCES WILL NEVER BECOME HOT ENOUGH TO BURN WHEN TOUCHED.

LEFT: A BUILT-IN WORK
SURFACE LIKE THIS ONE CAN
INCORPORATE TOY STORAGE,
ART MATERIALS, BOOKS
AND A DISPLAY AREA.
PROVIDE GOOD LIGHTING
AND A COMFORTABLE CHAIR
AND WATCH THE STANDARD
OF WORK SOAR.

BELOW: LOOK OUT FOR
SMALL SCHOOL DESKS IN
SECOND-HAND STORES –
THEY CAN BE REFRESHED
WITH A COAT OF PAINT AND
CHILDREN ADORE THEM.

Work Surfaces

In just the same way as the right tools help you to
do a job properly, a fully equipped work surface is
a real boon. Whether the task is changing
nappies, making animals from modelling clay, or
doing homework, it will seem much easier if you
are able to carry it out in comfort.

Before you actually have a baby, it is difficult to
imagine that you could change nappies often
enough to call it work and get backache from
doing it at the wrong height – but work it is, and
comfort is essential. If you have the space, it is
worth building or buying a special changing unit to
cater for all your needs. If you decorate the area
with mobiles, mirrors and toys to keep your baby
amused, changing time may even become more of
a pleasure than a chore.

ABOVE: A CHANGING UNIT LIKE THIS
WILL SPARE YOUR BACK. THERE'S A
PADDED MAT ON TOP AND SHELVES BELOW
FOR NAPPIES, WIPES, CREAMS, ETC.

BELOW: THIS COMPACT DESK WAS CUSTOM-BUILT
TO CATER FOR ALL THE TEENAGER'S NEEDS – FROM
HOMEWORK AND TELEVISION TO MUSIC AND
DESIGN. THE ANGLE-POISE LAMP IS PERFECT FOR
LIGHTING A CRAMPED CORNER SUCH AS THIS.

Toddlers love small tables and chairs where they can sit and snack, play or draw with their friends or a group of favourite teddies. If you feel the need to know which brand of child-sized furniture is the most robust, we suggest you visit a local playgroup to see what they use. Most pre-school children are very sociable and will prefer a shared table to a solitary desk.

SCHOOL AGE

Once your child starts school, a new set of standards apply. At school, everything is organized into different activity areas and most primary-age children enjoy this kind of structure and will appreciate having a small desk of their own, preferably an old-fashioned one with a lift-up lid to keep important things in. At this age, they are concerned for their work and their work surfaces should be taken seriously.

As your children grow up, their needs are less easy to generalize about and are more likely to be defined by their own interests. If your daughter is a computer whiz-kid, for example, she will need plenty of electrical sockets and a work surface deep enough to take a computer, keyboard and all the other related technology. If your son is a budding graphic designer, his ideal work surface will include a tilting drawing board, a good light and a place for his art materials and reference books.

BELOW: A SIMPLE CLIP-ON DEVICE LIKE THIS ONE FITS ANY DOOR TO PREVENT IT FROM SLAMMING SHUT. IT WILL SAVE YOUR CHILD'S FINGERS AND YOUR NERVES FROM TAKING A JOLT EVERY TIME YOU HEAR A DOOR BANG.

ABOVE: THESE PLASTIC GUARDS FIT ONTO THE SHARP CORNERS OF TABLES THAT, AT EXACTLY TODDLER HEAD-HEIGHT, CAN CAUSE A NASTY BUMP.

LEFT: STOP CHILDREN FALLING OUT OF WINDOWS BY FITTING THESE SECONDARY CATCHES NEAR THE TOP THAT ALLOW WINDOWS TO OPEN ONLY ENOUGH TO LET A BREEZE BLOW IN.

Safety

Common sense is the greatest safety device of all, and if you apply it when planning and decorating your children's rooms they should come to little harm. A lot of accidents happen because we don't appreciate our children's sharp learning curves – they see something being done, work out how, then try it themselves, all in half an hour!

THINK AHEAD
Babies can't take responsibility for their own well-being so we must think about safety more carefully than we did before we had them. This involves everything from fixing stair carpets and rugs so that we don't slip when carrying them to siting telephones in convenient places so that we don't have to run to answer them. Ensure that electric circuits, plugs and sockets are in good condition and fit your house with smoke alarms.

ABOVE: A LIGHT BROAD-BASED STOOL ENCOURAGES INDEPENDENCE. ACCIDENTS HAPPEN WHEN A CHILD IS TOO SMALL TO SEE WHAT HE IS REACHING FOR.

As soon as babies start to move around, they become capable of pulling themselves up and dragging things down from higher places, so watch out for trailing cables, table cloths and cupboard doors. If you have a staircase, fix gates at both ends, because crawlers love the challenge of an unguarded flight of stairs. When they reach toddler stage, look at the room from a child's height to see where the dangers lie: this way you can identify any blackspots – a sharp table corner, for example, which can be fitted with a self-adhesive cushion.

The most important safety aid for older children is education. Teach them about the dangers of fire, electricity, water and glass – so many accidents that happen to children could be avoided if they knew where the risks lurk.

BELOW: THIS SAFETY GATE EXPANDS TO FIT ANY DOORWAY AND INCLUDES A WALK-THROUGH GATE THAT ADULTS BUT NOT TODDLERS CAN NEGOTIATE.

Useful addresses

Accessories, toys and soft furnishings

Baby Basics
Tel: 01793 697 300

Mail order company selling toys and larger nursery play items.

BHS
129-137 Marylebone Road
London NW1 5QD

New mail order hotline number:
0990 247 000

Good range of coordinated cushions, throws and bedlinen.

Letterbox Catalogue
P.O. Box 114, Truro
Cornwall TR1 1FZ
Tel: 01872 580 885

Colourful selection of unusual small furniture, storage items and toys.

Beds and furniture

Bed in a Bag
81 Lower Bristol Road
Bath BA2 3BQ
Tel: 01225 334 445

Futon in a duffel bag - good guest bed for the Teenager's Room.

The Annabel Bevan Collection
Hand Painted Children's Furniture
44a Gwydr Crescent
Uplands, Swansea SA2 9JL
Tel: 01792 459 666

Specialize in beautiful hand-painted furniture for children.

Tim Chapman Setbuilding
2 Dunston Street
London E8 4EB
Tel: 0171 923 9909

Mail order for flatpack of bed used in the Little Girl's Room.

Full Moon Futons
Dept M.B., 20 Bulmershe Road
Reading RG1 5RJ
Tel: 0118 926 5648

Natural mattresses and futons for cots which conform to all appropriate safety standards.

Habitat
The Heal's Building
196 Tottenham Court Road
London W1P 9LD
Tel: 0171 255 2545

For nearest store telephone 0645 334 433. Seasonally changing children's ranges.

Harriet Anne Beds
Standen Farm, Smarden Road
Biddenden, Nr. Ashford
Kent TN27 8JT
Tel: 01580 291 220

Imported antique pine 'sleigh' beds; mattresses made to order; national delivery. Nice brochure.

IKEA
225 North Circular Road
London NW10 0JQ
Tel: 0181 208 5600

Good range of very reasonably priced children's furniture.

Joshua Jones Ltd
The Old Sawmill, Pamphill
Wimborne
Dorset BH21 4ED
Tel: 01202 888 821

Unique hand-made children's furniture.

Just Kidding
Stone Yard
Digbeth, Birmingham B12 0LX
Tel: 0121 624 0700

Mail order suppliers of many leading brands of furniture.

John Minter
Windmill Oast, Benenden Road
Rolvenden, Kent TN17 4PF
Tel: 01580 240 531

Child-sized hand-painted bedroom furniture.

Moriarti's Workshop
Ashford Road
High Halden, Nr. Ashford
Kent TN26 3LY
Tel: 01233 850 214

Solid pine storage beds.

Floors

Allied Carpets
Allied House, 76 High Street
Orpington, Kent BR6 0JQ
Tel: 0800 192 192

All carpets and wooden floors.

Crucial Trading Ltd
P.O. Box 11, Duke Place
Kidderminster DY10 2JR
Tel: 0171 730 0075

Produce natural floor coverings as carpet alternatives.

Forbo-Nairn Ltd
P.O. Box 1
Kirkcaldy, Fife
Scotland KY1 2SB
Tel: 0345 023 166

Produce versatile and hygienic cushioned floor coverings.

IKEA
Address as above.

Extensive range of unique carpets.

Thomas Lane Painted Interiors
57 Wellington Row
London E2 7BB
Tel: 0171 729 6195

Floors painted to commission.

Regency Wooden Floors of Brighton
The Timbers Industrial Unit
Vale Road, Portslade
Sussex BN41 1GG
Tel: 01273 430110

All brands of wooden floors.
National delivery and installation.

Wicanders
Amorim Ltd, Amorim House
Star Road, Partridge Green
Horsham
West Sussex RH13 8RA
Tel: 01403 710001

Corkfloor specialists – top quality
natural and coloured cork tiles.

Lighting

BHS
Address as above.

Well-deserved reputation for their
range of good, stylish and
reasonably priced lighting. Plenty
of bright, fun lamps for kids' rooms.

Habitat
Address as above.

Latest fashion looks; good basic
range.

Homebase
Beddington House
Railway Approach

Wallington
Surrey SM0 0HB
Tel: 0181 784 7200

Big lighting section in every store.
Good for basics.

IKEA
Address as above.

Special children's range where
safety features are paramount.

John Lewis
Oxford Street
London W1A 1EX
Tel: 0171 629 7711

Department store dependability.

Safety

John Lewis
Address as above.

Lovely baby and child departments;
all latest safety developments
alongside the standards.

Mothercare U.K. Ltd
Cherry Tree Road
Watford WD2 5SH
Tel: 01293 241 000

Definitive babycare and babywear
company; has a full range of safety
features for babies and young
children. Mail order service;
catalogue offers safety advice.

Tesco Direct Baby & Toddler
Catalogue
Tel: 0345 024 024

Really good catalogue with
everything from furniture to
clothing, including a good
selection of safety gates and
other gadgets.

Storage

Country Furniture
Dept I.H., 23 Bishops Wood
Nantwich
Cheshire CW5 7QD
Tel: 0120 610 543

Simple, inexpensive pine clothes
rails – as an alternative to chrome.

The Great Little Trading Company
124 Walcot Street
Bath BA1 5BG
Tel: 0990 673 008

Great for ideas on storage, as
well as other soft furnishing items.

The Holding Company
Unit 15, Imperial Studio
3-11 Imperial Road
London SW6 2AG
Tel: 0171 610 9160

Really innovative and exciting
storage ideas. Send for their
inspirational catalogue.

Homebase
Address as above.

Good quality DIY store with good
range of plastic storage systems.
Desks, swivel chairs, computer
desks and shelving systems.

IKEA
Address as above.

They have thought of everything –
all you need is stamina!

Lakeland Limited
Alexandra Buildings
Windermere
Cumbria LA23 1BQ
Tel: 01539 488 100

Range of home products. Storage Solutions catalogue has a good range of plastic and wicker baskets.

McCord Mail Order Catalogue
Tel: 0990 535 455

Painted wooden cupboards, wicker basket units, desks, shelving, underbed and other ingenious but stylish goodies.

Wall treatments

All main DIY chainstores carry a full range of safe paints suitable for use in children's rooms.

Brats Ltd
281 Kings Road
London SW3 5EW
Tel: 0171 351 7674

Mediterranean palette – a delicious range of paints in vibrant and soft chalky colours; colour charts and paints obtainable by mail order.

Roscolab Ltd
Blanchard Works
Kangley Bridge Road
London SE26 5AQ
Tel: 0181 659 2300

Rosco Supersaturated Paints as used in Toddler's Room; exceptionally vibrant colours that can be diluted 2:1 for opaque colours or 8:1 for colour wash.

Paint Magic
79 Shepperton Road
London N1 3DF
Tel: 0171 354 9696 (Courses and branch enquires); 0171 226 4420 (Mail order dept)

The shops sell paint, stencils, etc. Paint Magic also runs day courses in decorative paint techniques.

The Stencil Library
Stockfield Hall, Stockfield
Northumberland NE43 7TN
Tel: 01661 844 844

Ask for catalogue to discover their lovely range of stencils, paints and brushes. Mail order service.

Window treatments

The Finial Curtain Company
9 Netherby Road
London SE23 3AL
Tel: 0181 699 3626

Making up and fitting of most sorts of blinds.

Habitat
Address as above.

Inspirational catalogue with seasonal changes and lists of store locations. Great for ready-made funky curtains.

The House of Shutters
Studio 2
The Birches Business Centre
Selsey, Chichester
West Sussex PO20 9EP
Tel: 0171 610 4624

Interior shutters made to measure - for those who want the look we gave to the Teenager's Room without any DIY!

IKEA
Address as above.

Good fabric, curtain and blind ranges.

John Lewis
Address as above.

A really huge selection of curtain fabrics and accessories, plus curtain-making to order, ready-made blinds and kits.

Ian Mankin
109 Regent's Park Road
London NW1 8UR
Tel: 0171 722 099

Best-ever selection of natural fabrics – checks, stripes, ticking, etc. Mail order available.

Work surfaces

IKEA
Address as above.

Have a look at the current catalogue to cut down on your wandering-about time in the store. Plenty of adaptable worktops and drawer units.

STOMPA
The Old Mill House
Dockfield Road
Shipley
West Yorkshire BD17 7AE
Tel: 01274 596 885

A mid-priced range of solid pine furniture, such as space-saving bunks and desks.

The following major DIY chains will stock timber and laminates suitable for work surfaces:

B&Q
1 Hampshire Corporate Park
Chandlers Ford
Eastleigh
Hampshire FO53 3YX
Tel: 0181 466 4166

Do-It-All
Falcon House
The Minories
Dudley
West Midlands DY2 8PG
Tel: 0800 436 436

Homebase
Address as above.

Acknowledgements

Our thanks to Lorne and Roseanne Mitchell for allowing us to decorate baby Oscar's bedroom and to Miss Stephanie Casey; Roxy and Leo for letting us do up their rooms. We would also like to thank the ace photographer Bruce Hemming; top stylist Leeann Mackenzie and our carpenter Paul Roberts. And still more thanks to Gabrielle, Rona and Catherine for helping to make this project so much fun.

STOCKISTS CREDITS

Pages 12-17 Cot & bedlinen from Lilliput (The Nursery Shop), 225-259 Queenstown Rd, London SW8 3NP, tel: 0171 720 5554; chair & table from Shaker, 322 Kings Rd, London SW3 5UH, tel: 0171 352 3918; toys from Hamleys Ltd, 188-196 Regent Street, London W1R 6BT, tel: 0171 734 3161. Other stockists include: Baby World, 239 Munster Rd, London SW6 6BT, tel: 0171 386 1904; Little Bridge, 56 Battersea Bridge Rd, London SW11 3AG, tel: 0171 978 5522; The White Company, Unit 19C, The Coda Centre, 189 Munster Rd, London SW6 6AW, tel: 0171 385 7988; John Lewis Partnership, Oxford Street, London W1A 1EX, tel: 0171 629 7711. Pages 28-33 Table, sofa, chair, notice board & gerberas from IKEA, 2 Drury Way, North Circular Rd, London NW10 0TH, tel: 0181 208 5600; duvet cover etc from Habitat, The Heals Building, 196 Tottenham Court Rd, London W1P 9LD, tel: 0171 631 3880; toys from Hamleys Ltd, details as above & Tridias Toys, 25 Bute Street, London SW7 3EY, tel: 0171 584 2330; curtains from John Lewis Partnership, details as above. Other stockists include: The Holding Company, 245 Kings Rd, London SW3 5EL, tel: 0171 610 9160; The Pier, 200 Tottenham Court Rd, London W1P 0AD, tel: 0171 637 7704. Pages 42-7 Bedlinen, trunk, birdcage, chest of drawers & hand basket from Tobias & the Angel, 68 White Hart Lane, London SW13 0P2, tel: 0181 878 8902; Picture frames from The Pier, details as above; baskets from The Holding Company, details as above; flooring & carpets from IKEA, details as above. Other stockists include: Damask, 3-4 Broxholme House, New Kings Rd, London SW6 4AA, tel: 0171 731 3553. Pages 56-61 Bed, chair, table & clothes rail from Habitat, details as above; stainless steel storage from Muji, 26 Great Marlborough Street, London W1V 1HL, tel: 0171 494 1197. Other stockists include: IKEA, details as above.

The authors and publishers would also like to thank the following companies for supplying goods used in this book:
Clements of St Leonards (curtains and blinds for the Little Girl's Room), 55 London Rd, St Leonards-on-Sea, East Sussex TA37 6AY, tel: 01424 423 570; Electrolux Leisure Appliances (black fridge for the Teenager's Room), P.O. Box 88, Oakley Rd, Luton, Bedfordshire LU4 9QQ, tel: 01582 588 468; Lakeland Ltd (jelly boxes in the Toddler's Room), Alexandra Buildings, Windermere, Cumbria LA23 1BQ, tel: 01539 488 100.

PICTURE CREDITS

BBC Books would like to thank the following for providing photographs and for permission to reproduce copyright material. While every effort has been made to trace and acknowledge all copyright holders, we would like to apologize should there have been any errors or omissions.
Pages 12 (b), 28 (b), 42 (b) & 56 (b) by Shona Wood © BBC. All other photography by Bruce Hemming © BBC.

Page 71 (tl, bl & br) IKEA, (tr) Mothercare; Page 72 IKEA; Page 73 (t) Robert Harding Picture Library (Dominic Blackmore/Homes & Ideas), (br) Robert Harding Picture Library (Bill Reavell/Homes & Ideas); Page 74 IKEA; Page 75 (t) Robert Harding Picture Library (Andreas von Einsiedel/Homes & Gardens), (b) IKEA; Page 76 IKEA; Page 77 (tr) Elizabeth Whiting & Assocs (Rodney Hyett), (cl & br) Forbo Nairn; Page 78 (bl) The Interior Archive (Fritz von der Schulenburg); Page 79 (l) Robert Harding Picture Library (James Merrell/Homes & Gardens), (tr) Robert Harding Picture Library (T. Orme/Ideal Home), (br) The Interior Archive (Simon Brown); Pages 80 and 81 (t) Mothercare; Page 81 (b) Robert Harding Picture Library (Dominic Blackmore/Homes & Ideas); Page 82 Robert Harding Picture Library (Bill Reavell/Homes & Ideas); Page 83 (t) IKEA, (cr) Robert Harding Picture Library (Ian Skelton/Homes & Ideas); Page 84 (tl) IKEA, (cr) Robert Harding Picture Library (Ian Skelton/Homes & Ideas); Page 85 (tr) The Great Little Trading Company, (cl) IKEA, (b) Elizabeth Whiting & Assocs (Shona Wood); Page 86 (tr) Robert Harding Picture Library (Dominic Blackmore/Homes & Ideas); Page 87 (t) Robert Harding Picture Library (David Giles/Homes & Ideas), (bl) IKEA, (br) The Great Little Trading Company; Page 88 (tl) IKEA, (br) The Annabel Bevan Collection; Page 89 (tl) IKEA; Page 90 (sp) Mothercare, (cr & bl) IKEA; Page 91 (r & bl) IKEA.

MDF PRECAUTIONS

The safety of this material has been brought into question recently. Any danger is thought to arise from the inhalation of dust coming from the sawing or sanding of MDF. This is related to the materials and methods used in its manufacture. When using MDF the following precautions are advised. Always saw and sand MDF outside in the open air. Never do so in a a carpeted room because the dust is too fine to be removed by a household vacuum cleaner. Always wear a suitable breathing mask when working with MDF. Seal the surface of MDF with a coat of paint or varnish. If you would prefer to use another material, we suggest plywood, which comes in a range of thicknesses and has similar qualities.

Index

A acrylic glaze, making, 50
alcove, making use of, 39
angle-poise lamp, 87
appliqué, 17
appliquéd curtains, 20-3

B baby changer, 15
Baby's Room, 7-8, 12-27
bamboo blinds, 81
bed vs bunk, 75
beds, 72-5
bedside light, choosing, 87
blackout blinds, 47
blinds, choices of, 80-1
built-in cupboards, 82
built-in work surface, 88

C cabin beds, 75
carpet vs other flooring, 76
chalkboard, 31
changing unit, 88
  making, 26-7
chimney breast, making use of, 82
choosing a theme:
  for teenagers, 58-9
  for toddlers, 32
coat hangers, decorated, 84
colourwashing, 17
  background, 18
  painting, 53
contract carpeting, 76
cork tiles, 76
corner sink, decorating, 48
cot bumper, 15
cot-beds, 75
cots, 72
cradles, 72
cupboard, 38-9
cupboards, adapting, 45
curtaining, with a staple gun, 81
curtains:
  appliquéd, 20-3
  choices of, 80-1
  sink, 48-9
cushioned vinyl flooring, 77

D day bed, 61

decorative themes, 44
dimmer switches, 17, 33, 86
dressing table stool, upholstered,
  8, 54-5

E electrical sockets, 89

F fabric, choosing, 17
floor coverings, 47
floors, 76-7
foam stamp, making, 34-5
folding screen, 15
frieze, hand-painted, 50-1
furniture, for young children, 44-5

L lambskin fleeces, 15
lighting:
  general, 86-7
  in a baby's room, 17
  in a toddler's room, 33
  lining fabrics, 80
Little Girl's Room, 42-55
louvred doors, adapting, 62

M matching bedding, 80
Moses baskets, 72
murals, 17

N night lights, 87

P paint, diluting, 17
paper blinds, 81
patchwork, 17
patchwork wall, 34-5
peg rails:
  for teenagers, 58
  making, for toddlers, 36
pinboards:
  making, for Teenager's Room, 64-7
  making, for Toddler's Room, 8, 37
plaid wall, painting, 52-3
plastic corner guards, 90
platform bed, 73

S safety 90-1
safety gate, 91
safety, with lighting, 86-7

screen, making, 24-5
shelving systems, 84
shutters:
  fitting, 63
  painting, 62
sink curtains, 48-9
softboard, fixing to wall, 64
sponge roller, customizing, 52
sponge stamped design, 16, 18-19
spotlights, 17, 33
stencilled floor, 77
stencilling, 78, 79
storage, 82-5
  boxes, 82-3
  for toddlers, 31
  for young children, 44-5
  for teenagers, 68-9
striplights, 33
swag template, making, 50-1
swatches, collecting fabric, 58

T table lamps, 33
  decorating, 33
Teenager's Room, 9, 56-69
tie-backs:
  from fabric, 81
  from MDF, 81
Toddler's Room, 8, 28-41

V variable lighting, 86
Venetian blinds, 81
vinyl tiles, 76

W wall treatments:
  Baby's Room, 18-19
  Little Girl's Room, 50-3
  Toddler's Room, 34-5
wall-mounted lights, 33
walls, 78-9
  washable finishes, 78
wicker baskets, as storage, 14, 45
window catches, 90
window shutters, 62-3
windows, 80-1
wiring, 86
work surfaces, 88-9
worktop, customizing, 66-7